From Hohokam to O'odham

The Protohistoric Occupation of the
Middle Gila River Valley, Central Arizona

ii

A draft of this volume of the Gila River Indian Community, Anthropological Research Papers was previously distributed by the Cultural Resource Management Program as P-MIP Technical Report No. 2002-14.

Gila River Indian Community
Anthropological Research Papers
Number 3

From Hohokam to O'odham

The Protohistoric Occupation of the Middle Gila River Valley, Central Arizona

E. Christian Wells

Gila River Indian Community
Cultural Resource Management Program
Sacaton, Arizona

About the Author

E. CHRISTIAN WELLS, Ph.D., is Assistant
Professor of Anthropology at the University
of South Florida, Tampa, FL 33620

Cover: Detail from Eusebio Francis
Kino's map of southern and central Arizona
(1701–1702), showing his record of
communities encountered during his travels
among the "Sobaiporis" of the San Pedro
River. The map shows the location of "Casa
Grande" on the "R. Hila" in the upper right-
hand corner, along with Mission San Xavier
and the community of "Quburi," or Quiburi,
near the confluence of the Babocomari
River. (Courtesy of Special Collections,
University of Arizona Library)

Printed in the United States of America

ISBN 978 0-9723347-2-3

Second printing, 2009

TABLE OF CONTENTS

List of Figures

x

List of Tables

xii

FOREWORD

The variability that characterizes the archaeological record of the Hohokam and the historical documentation of the Akimel O'odham in the middle Gila River valley has been of interest to scholars studying man's adaptation to the Sonoran Desert for more than a century. Were the Hohokam the ancestors of the modern-day O'odham? Or, do the sharp contrasts in population levels, organization, and settlements—irrigation networks, ballcourts and platform mounds versus dispersed *rancherias* and ditch irrigation—indicate the presence of different cultural groups?

The late Emil Haury suggested that the archaeological data required to bridge the gap (A.D. 1450 to 1700) in our knowledge between the prehistoric Hohokam and historic Akimel O'odham or Pima lies buried in archaeological survey collections. Identifying contexts and material remains that represent the protohistoric period—the transition between the prehistoric Hohokam and historic Akimel O'odham or Pima Indians—continues to elude archaeologists working in central Arizona. The full-coverage survey of 146,000 acres of the Gila River Indian Community for the Pima-Maricopa Irrigation Project provides a massive data set to investigate Haury's hunch. Two-hundred and one so-called Sobaipuri and/or Historic Pima points were recovered from the surface of 48 sites (Leondorf and Rice 2004). For the most part, these points were collected from multi-component sites containing both prehistoric and historic assemblages.

This volume by Christian Wells seeks to identify new approaches for detecting and studying sites along the middle Gila River valley that contain protohistoric assemblages. Wells reviews the evidence for protohistoric settlement in central Arizona, introduces quantitative measures to identify pottery assemblages, and suggests potential avenues for future research. His study represents the Gila River Indian Community, Cultural Resource Management Program's first step in identifying sites that are potential candidates for further investigations needed to develop a diagnostic set of material traits for the Protohistoric period.

John C. Ravesloot, Coordinator
Cultural Resource Management Program

ACKNOWLEDGMENTS

The work presented here was carried out by the Gila River Indian Community's Cultural Resource Management Program (CRMP) in association with the Pima-Maricopa Irrigation Project (P-MIP). I gratefully acknowledge the aid and support of E. Lee Thompson, Director of the P-MIP, and John C. Ravesloot, Coordinator of the CRMP. The P-MIP was developed by the Gila River Indian Community, resulting from the community's administration of U.S. Bureau of Reclamation, Department of Interior funds under the Tribal Self-Governance Act of 1994 (P.L. 103-413), for the design and development of a water delivery system utilizing Central Arizona Project water. The CRMP was established by the community to address the impacts of the irrigation project on cultural resources.

I would like to thank Patricia L. Crown, William H. Doelle, Paul R. Fish, Keith W. Kintigh, Teresita Majewski, and John C. Ravesloot for their comments on drafts of this paper. I also would like to express my gratitude to George L. Cowgill, J. Andrew Darling, Karla L. Davis-Salazar, B. Sunday Eiselt, Ruth L. Greenspan, Chris Loendorf, Derek P. Morgan, Brenda G. Randolph, Glen E. Rice, Bonny Rockette-Wagner, Teresa L. Rodrigues, Arleyn W. Simon, and M. Kyle Woodson for their advice and guidance on aspects of the project's research design as well as interpretation of the results. Rebecca J. Waugh generously shared her research on early historic pottery of the Tucson area, and Margaret E. Beck provided helpful information on recent protohistoric research in the Tucson Basin. Many thanks to Lynn Simon for drafting the maps that appear as Figures 1, 4, and 7. Tom Herrschaft took great care in producing the final document.

CHAPTER 1

THE ARCHAEOLOGY
OF THE PROTOHISTORIC PERIOD

. . . we are still floundering in our efforts to close the gap from about
A.D. 1450 to A.D. 1700. . . . Willingness to look for the less obvious
and learning to recognize undramatic remains will surely bring the two
ends of the story together. I suspect that the data may already be on
hand, buried in survey materials. . . .

Emil Walter Haury
Thoughts after Sixty Years as a Southwestern Archaeologist

Archaeologists working in the American Southwest typically refer to the time of
transition between prehistory and history as the Protohistoric, from roughly A.D. 1450 to
1700, although the reported dates for this period range widely (e.g., Adams and Duff 1985;
Bronitsky 1985; Cable 1990; Doelle 1984; Doelle and Wallace 1990; Goodyear 1977;
McGuire 1982). Originally, the Pecos Classification of 1927 labeled the era, "Pueblo IV, or
proto-Historic" (Roberts 1935:8), and Gladwin and Gladwin (1935:256–259) referred to this
time as the "Bachi Phase" of Southwest Prehistory. Since these early studies, many
archaeologists have used the term "Protohistoric," although only a few have given serious
consideration to its diagnostic characteristics (e.g., Di Peso 1953; Gilpin and Phillips 1998;
Ravesloot and Whittlesey 1987; Riley 1987; Wilcox and Masse 1981).

From these and other studies, we know that the fifteenth through seventeenth
centuries marked an interval of cultural transformation of great magnitude, representing a
critical juncture of reorganization of peoples on a massive scale—a process that appears to
have coursed for over 200 years. In central Arizona, the period encompasses the poorly
understood transition from the prehistoric Hohokam to the historically documented
O'odham, from large villages with complex hydraulic facilities to small homesteads whose
inhabitants relied on dry-farming and flood-water agriculture, and from extensive trade
networks articulating peoples and resources from large portions of the Southwest and
northern and western Mexico to localized economies shaped by short-distance exchanges
among widely dispersed groups.

Yet, despite its importance to Southwest prehistory, there is a notable lack of detailed
information regarding the Protohistoric, especially in central Arizona. While comprehensive
studies have been published on early Spanish documentary sources that describe the later part
of this era (e.g., Doelle 1981, 1984; Ezell 1961, 1983; Gilpin and Phillips 1998; Masse 1981;
Reff 1991; Riley 1987; Wilson 1999; Winter 1973), archaeological data, because they are so

sparse, have received little systematic attention. As Haury remarks in the above quotation, since Protohistoric remains tend to be "less obvious" and "undramatic," archaeologists continue to struggle with understanding the time-space systematics of post-Hohokam cultural trajectories.

The aim of this study is to determine ways of detecting and studying Protohistoric sites and deposits along the middle Gila River Valley, with the greater goal of identifying significant research questions that can be addressed with these data. Above, Haury suggests that survey data likely hold important information on the Protohistoric, although we need to fine-tune our analytical lenses to see it. The Gila River Indian Community's Cultural Resource Management Program has been conducting a full-coverage archaeological survey of large contiguous blocks of terrain along both sides of the Gila River, from the confluence of the Gila and Salt rivers in the west to the Santan Mountains in the east, covering over 525 km^2 (Figure 1). As a result, over 1,000 sites, spanning the Middle Archaic through the Historic time periods, have been recorded, mapped, and surface collected (Ravesloot and Waters 2004). Given the broad time scale represented by this settlement, these survey data potentially could yield clues to identifying Protohistoric occupations and to understanding the organizational strategies of groups occupying the region prior to the arrival of the Spanish.

In this study, I briefly review the archaeological evidence for Protohistoric settlement in central Arizona, highlighting some of the challenges that confront researchers and suggesting potential avenues for future research. This overview reveals that a fundamental problem is the identification of Protohistoric occupations when they are integrated into multiple-component sites that include prehistoric and historic remains. A related problem with broader significance is the determination of when the Protohistoric period begins in this region, which has important implications for modeling the reorganization of Hohokam society at the end of the Classic period, from about A.D. 1350 to 1450.

I next turn my attention to the middle Gila River Valley, where I summarize what we know about the Protohistoric from Spanish reports and historical information, as well as what we can infer from extant archaeological evidence. I then introduce a set of quantitative measures for identifying Protohistoric pottery assemblages. Here, I compare ceramic assemblage data produced from excavations of prehistoric and historic sites from central Arizona against ceramic data from multiple-component sites along the middle Gila to determine if Protohistoric remains can be detected. I combine multivariate quantitative measures to examine pottery assemblages from Classic, Polvorón phase, and Historic sites in the Phoenix Basin, along with those from the middle Gila, which I suspect contain evidence for Protohistoric occupation. These exercises thus set up a method for detecting potential Protohistoric occupations in multiple-component sites using survey data. Based on the results of these preliminary investigations of surface collections, I suggest a few ways to evaluate these findings using more detailed studies that examine larger data sets.

The difficulty in defining and documenting the social and material expressions of populations from this period is partly a result of the paucity of archaeological evidence, and partly because indigenous groups experienced European influences at different times and

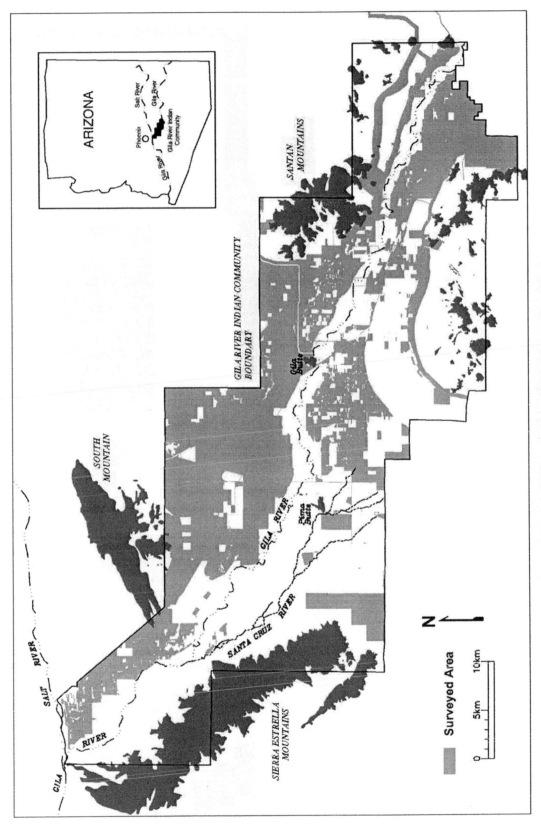

Figure 1. The Gila River Indian Community showing area surveyed.

places throughout the region (Bronitsky 1985:139; Reff 1992; Riley 1987:15–29; Wilcox and Masse 1981:14). It is often difficult to disentangle evidence of Protohistoric occupation from that of early Historic times. It is equally challenging to differentiate Protohistoric features, deposits, and artifacts from those generated during late Classic times. Below, I review the archaeological evidence for the Protohistoric period in central Arizona from two perspectives: the transition from prehistory (about A.D. 1450) and the transition to history (about A.D. 1700). Understanding the prehistoric and historic context of the peoples that occupied the Hohokam region during the Protohistoric is necessary for developing inferences about the period's cultural systems and for determining the test implications with which those inferences can be evaluated.

THE TRANSITION FROM PREHISTORY

Archaeologists are in general agreement that the Protohistoric period begins sometime after the Civano phase of the Classic period, from roughly A.D. 1300 to 1450 (Dean 1991:91; see also Henderson and Martynec 1993; Marmaduke and Henderson 1995), although these dates vary as much as 50 to 100 years from region to region (compare chapters in Gumerman 1991 and Gumerman 1994). Useful syntheses of the Civano phase Hohokam can be found in Bayman (2001:280–290), Doyel (1991:253–258), and Fish (1989:31–34). Hohokam society during this period is characterized by a hierarchy of settlement types, including villages with only one or a few walled residential compounds encompassing post-reinforced and adobe-walled structures, and settlements with one or more platform mound compounds, as well as other compounds (Doyel 1980:37). As in the preceding Soho phase, settlement remained strategically positioned among irrigation canals along the Salt, Gila, Santa Cruz, and San Pedro rivers (Fish et al. 1992; Gregory and Nials 1985; Howard 1987; Rice 1998a). At this time, large settlements, such as Casa Grande, contained one or more platform mounds, numerous residential compounds, and a tower or Great House (Wilcox and Shenk 1977).

These types of Classic period settlements have been postulated to form distinct irrigation communities—sociopolitical organizations consisting of a series of integrated villages distributed along a single canal or within a canal system, which included one or more platform mound villages that served as administrative centers (Gregory 1991; Howard 1987). Some platform mounds appear to have evolved in function from special, nonresidential facilities to residences used by certain segments of society in the Civano phase (Doelle 1995; Doelle et al. 1995; Doyel 1974, 1981; Elson 1998; Elson and Abbott 2000; Gregory 1987). These developments may reflect increasing social differentiation and possibly the existence of elite groups controlling and coordinating ritual and agricultural knowledge (e.g., Doyel 1991; Wilcox 1991; (Wilcox and Shenk 1977).

Doyel (1991:262) notes that increased variability in mortuary programs that diverged from earlier traditions, along with "increasingly restricted social space, increased storage space in some sites, the continued incorporation of some canal systems, and the hierarchical structure of settlement systems" all suggest a pattern of expanding social differentiation. In addition, some scholars (e.g., Graybill and Nials 1989; Graybill et al. 1999; Huckleberry 1999; Nials et al. 1989; compare Waters and Ravesloot 2001) have argued that the Civano phase represents a period of prolonged drought followed by massive floods, which seriously impacted subsistence practices and settlement. Still others argue that warfare (e.g., LeBlanc 1999; Rice 2001; Wallace and Doelle 2001) and European-introduced diseases (e.g., Fink 1991; Reff 1990, 1992; Roberts and Ahlstrom 1997) had serious consequences for Hohokam demography and social organization. Within the context of this dynamic social and ecological climate, the Classic Hohokam cultural traditions soon changed dramatically as these communities reorganized themselves in a radically different way (see Abbott 2003).

Sires's (1984) work at the site of El Polvorón in the Queen Creek drainage in the eastern portion of the Phoenix Basin produced materials that he believes represent a "post-Civano Hohokam occupation" dating between A.D. 1350 and 1450 or later, which he calls the "Polvorón phase" (see also Crown and Sires 1984). At El Polvorón, this phase is distinguished from the prior Civano phase of the Classic period by a dramatic shift in settlement from large, aggregated communities marked by adobe compounds to small, dispersed groups of single-unit jacal pit houses. Distinctiveness in terms of material culture, compared to the preceding Civano phase, is expressed in different artifact frequencies rather than types. Changes in ceramic inventories, for example, include decreased proportions of red-on-buff ceramics, and increased proportions of Salt and Gila red wares and Salado polychromes relative to Civano phase assemblages, along with the appearance of intrusive types, namely proto-Hopi yellow wares (Bidahochi Polychrome and Jeddito Black-on-yellow), San Carlos Red-on-brown, and Tanque Verde Red-on-brown pottery.

As independent supporting evidence for the definition of the Polvorón phase, Sires (1984) cites one calibrated radiocarbon date (A.D. 1410 to 1650) from "architectural elements" and one adjusted archaeomagnetic date (A.D. 1400 to 1450) from a "structure hearth." In addition, Sires (1984:316–324) notes similarities of the materials from El Polvorón with those from terminal occupations at other sites in the region, namely Compound F at Casa Grande (Hayden 1957), Las Colinas (Hammack and Sullivan 1981), Escalante Ruin (Doyel 1974), Los Muertos (Haury 1945), and AZ U:13:22 near Snaketown (Haury 1976). However, not all archaeologists agree with Sires's comparative examples (Andresen 1985; Doyel 1991:263; Hackbarth 1995; Henderson and Hackbarth 2000).

Since Sires's original publication of the El Polvorón data, archaeologists have made attempts to identify Polvorón phase occupations at archaeological sites in central and southern Arizona, mainly in the Phoenix Basin (e.g., Abbott et al. 1994; Andresen 1985; Bostwick and Downum 1994; Bostwick et al. 1996; Chenault 1993, 1996, 2000; Crown and Sires 1984; Doyel 1991, 1995; Foster 1994; Greenwald and Ciolek-Torello 1988; Gregory 1988; Henderson 1995; Howard 1988; Howell 1993; Mitchell 1994; Teague 1988). Some of the diagnostic traits most often used to infer the presence of Polvorón phase settlements are derived from those enlisted to describe the Protohistoric in general (Table 1).

Chenault (1993, 1996, 2000) and Hackbarth (1995; see also Henderson and Hackbarth 2000) provide the most recent summaries of extant Polvorón data that shape these

Table 1. Diagnostic Criteria for Identifying Protohistoric Settlement.

Proposed Traits	References
Settlement Pattern	
ranchería-style settlement pattern	Doelle 1981; Ezell 1961, 1983; Garrett and Russell 1983; Gilpin and Phillips 1998; Kisselburg 1989; Layhe 1986; McKenna and Swarthout 1984; Rice et al. 1983; Wilson 1999; Winter 1973
jacal-style residential structures	Doyel 1974; Hammack and Sullivan 1981; Haury 1945, 1976; Hayden 1957; Kisselburg 1989; Layhe 1986; Masse 1990; McKenna and Swarthout 1984; Ravesloot et al. 1992; Rice et al. 1983; Sires 1984; Wenker et al. 1996; Wilson 1999
Material Culture	
high assemblage proportions of Salt and Gila Red wares and low proportions of buff wares relative to Civano assemblages	Abbott 1994; Abbott et al. 1994; Andresen 1985; Bostwick and Downum 1994; Bostwick et al. 1996; Chenault 1993, 1996, 2000; Crown and Sires 1984; Doyel 1991, 1995; Foster 1994; Greenwald and Ciolek-Torrello 1988; Gregory 1988; Henderson 1995a; Howard 1988; Howell 1993; Mitchell 1994, 1996; Newman and Woodson 2002; Sires 1984; Teague 1988
increasing assemblage proportions of Salado Polychromes	Abbott 1994; 2000; Chenault 1993, 1996, 2000; Crown 1981, 1994; Danson and Wallace 1956; Dittert and Plog 1980; Simon et al. 1998; Sires 1984
appearance of intrusive Hopi Jeddito Black-on-Yellow, Zuni Matsaki Polychrome, and Lower Colorado Buff ware ceramics	Bayman and Ryan 1988; Deaver 1990; Wenker et al. 1996
appearance of Sobaipuri Plain and Whetstone Plain pottery	Bronitsky and Merritt 1986; Di Peso 1951, 1953; Doelle 1984; Doyel 1977; Downum 1993; Downum et al. 1986; Fontana 1965; Fontana and Matson 1987; Franklin 1980; Fritz 1989; Gerald 1968; Grebinger 1976; Huckell 1984; Masse 1981; Ravesloot and Whittlesey 1987; Wallace and Holmlund 1986; Wilcox 1987
appearance of Pima Plain, Pima Red, and Pima Red-on-buff pottery	Deaver 1990; Douglas 1953; Drucker 1941; Gasser et al. 1990; Haury 1976; Hayden 1959; Kisselburg 1989; Layhe 1986; Rice et al. 1983; Russell 1908; Wenker et al. 1996; Wood 1987:114
use of quartz- and feldspar-rich sand for ceramic paste temper	Abbott 1994; Cable and Gould 1988; Cable and Mitchell 1988; Crown 1981; Deaver 1990; Henderson 1995b; Newman and Woodson 2002; Walsh-Anduze 1993, 1996a, 1996b
increase in assemblage proportions of obsidian	Chenault 1993; Landis 1990; Sires 1984
appearance of Sobaipuri-style projectile points	Ayres 1971; Brew and Huckell 1987; Di Peso 1951, 1953, 1956, 1958, 1981; Doelle 1984; B. Huckell 1980, 1984; L. Huckell 1981; Loendorf and Rice 2002; Masse 1981; Ravesloot and Whittlesey 1987; Simpson and Wells 1983
decrease in the importation of marine shell	Sires 1984; Vokes 1984

traits, although the two researchers offer widely different interpretations of their significance. Chenault (1993:137) contends that the differences observed between Classic and post-Classic excavated sites represent a significant cultural change that is distinguishable from the Civano phase based on architectural style and the content of artifact assemblages. "The Hohokam post-Classic period was a time of reduced population, simplified social structure, a more dispersed settlement pattern, a simplified agricultural production system involving less irrigation, simplified architectural construction and crafts production, and a probable change in ritual practices." In contrast, Hackbarth (1995:174) argues that the archaeological evidence can be interpreted as variation between contemporaneous late Classic features resulting, in part, from a geographically uneven decline in population:

> During a period of declining population, changes in material culture may represent accommodations to the harsh realities of survival, not modification of cultural behaviors. In other words, as the number of options available to a population declines, the *appearance* of cultural change may increase. However, instead of changing behaviors, the appearance may simply be a shift in the relative frequencies of artifacts being used by mainstream or fringe elements of the group. Demographic change does not automatically translate into social changes.

Whether the Polvorón phase represents a new set of cultural traditions replacing an older one or reflects behavioral adaptations in the context of demographic decline, it is clear that the pace of Hohokam change at this time was continuous, albeit variable, across different geographic areas in the Sonoran Desert (see Abbott 2003). As a result, efforts to identify Polvorón phase artifacts and deposits in the archaeological record have met with limited success, particularly because absolute dates (i.e., radiocarbon and archaeomagnetic assays) recovered from excavated materials have been found to overlap significantly with late Classic samples (e.g., Abbott et al. 1994; Ahlstrom et al. 1995; Doyel 1995; Henderson and Hackbarth 2000; Howell 1993:145–147; Marmaduke and Henderson 1995:137; Murphy et al. 1984; Zyniecki 1993). Further, there have been no clear diagnostic artifacts to signal features or deposits that were produced during this phase. Given these challenges, perhaps the question to pose, as Hackbarth (1995:175) asks, "is not whether the terms 'Civano' or 'Polvorón' correctly describe this area, but rather, 'What is this phenomenon that postdates A.D. 1350, and does it signal a significant social change from earlier periods?'" In other words, while there is substantial variability in material patterning during the late Classic, do cultural units in the Polvorón phase exhibit sufficient behavioral integrity to render them archaeologically distinct from Classic Hohokam groups?

THE TRANSITION TO HISTORY

Just as there is lengthy debate over the shift from prehistory, there is considerable disagreement about the transition to history. In southern Arizona, the end of the Protohistoric period sometimes is defined in relation to the arrival of Europeans, beginning with the travels of Álvar Nuñez Cabeza de Vaca in 1536 (Hallenbeck 1940). Early Spanish contact with indigenous populations was sporadic, however, until the late seventeenth century when Father Eusebio Kino and others began making regular visits to the area (Bolton 1948; see also Riley 1976). Since interactions between Spaniards and indigenous groups were intermittent and limited at first, most archaeologists and historians set the endpoint of the Protohistoric period at roughly 1700 (see Whittlesey 1996:72–80), although a few have argued against the use of this period altogether or else have limited it to 1536 (e.g., Cordell 1984; Di Peso 1981; Fontana 1965; McGregor 1965).

Comprehensive studies of early Spanish documentary materials provide the greatest details for the period (e.g., Doelle 1981, 1984; Ezell 1961, 1983; Gilpin and Phillips 1998; Masse 1981; Reff 1991; Riley 1987; Wilson 1999; Winter 1973). Cable (1990:23.14–23.45) provides a brief, but generally complete, overview of these sources and summarizes their implications for late seventeenth and early eighteenth century political geography. According to Spanish texts, there were a number of Piman-speaking populations, including the Pima along the headwaters of the Altar and Santa Cruz rivers, the Sobaipuri of the Santa Cruz and San Pedro rivers, the Gileño who lived along the middle Gila River, the Papago of southern Arizona, and the Soba of the San Ignacio River and Gulf Coast of California (Bolton 1948:346–348). Later, some of these groups reorganized into the modern Akimel O'odham (Pima), Tohono O'odham (Papago), and Pee-Posh (Maricopa; Wilson 1999:1.4).

The Spanish captain Juan Mateo Manje (Bolton 1948:196), who explored portions of southern Arizona with Kino in the late seventeenth century, notes that the Pima lived in scattered settlements that contained no more than 2,000 inhabitants, were spread out among 5 to 10 locations, and extended for 53 mi ("21 leagues") from the vicinity of the Casa Grande monument to the confluence of the Gila and Salt rivers (Figure 2). Generally, populations appear to have ranged in number from a few hundred to a few thousand across southern and central Arizona (Dobyns 1963:164, 180–181; Doelle 1984:203–204).

Settlement took the form of a *ranchería*-style pattern, consisting of extended-family households (clusters of houses, called *ki:kĭ*), each of which was self-sufficient and politically autonomous (Doelle 1981:65–66; Ezell 1983:151). Pima homes (*ki*) were domed jacal structures built over a square frame of large posts and beams (Figure 3); walls were composed of branches and reeds covered with earth (Garrett and Russell 1983; e.g., Kisselburg 1989; Layhe 1986; McKenna and Swarthout 1984; Masse 1990; Upham 1983). A number of extramural features often were associated with the *ki*, including ramadas (*vaptto*), brush kitchens (*u'uksha*), and storage structures (*koksin*; Rea 1997:146). Subsistence strategies involved limited *ak-chin* (hillslope run-off) farming for the cultivation of corn, beans, pumpkins, watermelons, muskmelons, and cotton, supplemented by hunting and gathering (Castetter and Bell 1942; Hackenberg 1983). However, the Franciscan friar Marcos de Niza observed irrigation agriculture in the Santa Cruz Valley or San Pedro Valley in 1539 (Hammond and Rey 1940:70; see also Ezell 1961).

While many details on late Protohistoric and early Historic lifeways can be obtained from the Spanish narratives (e.g., Riley 1976), archaeological remains from the period are poorly known (see Majewski and Ayres 1997; Whittlesey 1996). Further, it is difficult to

Figure 2. Detail from Eusebio Francis Kino's map of southern and central Arizona (1701–1702), showing his record of communities encountered during his travels among the "Sobaiporis" of the San Pedro River. This is the English engraving of the manuscript map, published in 1762 and derived from the first publication, in French, in 1705. The map shows the location of "Casa Grande" on the "R. Hila" in the upper right-hand corner, along with Mission San Xavier and the community of "Quburi," or Quibliri, near the confluence of the Babocomari River. (Courtesy of Special Collections, University of Arizona Library; 1701. Eusebio Francisco Kino. Passage by land to California. Discover'd by Father Eusebius Francis Kino, a Jesuit; Between the Years 1698 & 1701: Containing Likewise the New Missions of the Jesuits. E. Bowen Sc., London, 1762. Map 24 x 21 cm. Scale ca, 1:5,100,000. From Jesuits, Letters from Missions, Travels of the Jesuits, by John Lockman. 2d ed. corr. London, 1762, vol. 1, opposite page 395. [G4301 S1 1762 K5].)

derive testable implications for identifying Protohistoric groups from Spanish sources and modern ethnographies, because historic populations are defined on the basis of shared language and kinship, while prehistoric populations are defined on the basis of shared material culture traditions. Detailed studies of historic material culture patterning are thus necessary for developing criteria for identifying Protohistoric settlements.

Figure 3. An example of a nineteenth century Pima *ki* (house). There are four large posts forming a central support framework. Smaller branches were placed around the central frame. The *ki* was then covered with grass and, in some parts, with a layer of earth. Photo courtesy of the Gila River Indian Community.

Work by Di Peso (1951, 1953, 1956, 1958) in the 1940s and 1950s at several suspected early historic period and Spanish contact sites in the San Pedro (Quiburi, Santa Cruz de Gaybanipitea, Babocomari Village, Reeve Ruin, Davis Ranch, and Solas Ranch) and Santa Cruz river valleys (Paloparado) produced abundant information regarding Pima material culture, which enabled him to make inferences about settlement organization, mortuary programs, and production and subsistence economies. Figure 2 shows the suspected locations of some of these communities. Ravesloot and Whittlesey (1987:83–90) provide a thorough overview of Di Peso's findings (see also Cable 1990; Di Peso 1981; Masse 1981).

Importantly, during his excavations at Quiburi, Di Peso (1951, 1953) identified two plain ware pottery types—"Sobaipuri Plain" (a thick, poorly polished ware with sand and organic temper) and "Whetstone Plain" (a much thinner, hand-smoothed ware with a sandy, bumpy finish)—and a unique triangular projectile point style with a concave base and serrated edges, all of which he recognized as part of the utilitarian toolkits of early historic Sobaipuri groups of the Santa Cruz and San Pedro valleys. While numerous inconsistencies have been pointed out with regards to Di Peso's initial inferences (Bronitsky and Merritt 1986; Cable 1990; Cheek 1974; Doyel 1977; Fontana 1965; Fontana and Matson 1987; Fritz

1989; Gerald 1968; Grebinger 1976; Masse 1981; Ravesloot and Whittlesey 1987; Seymour 1989; Shenk and Teague 1975; Wheat 1956; Wilcox 1987; Williams 1986), the definition of these two pottery types and one projectile point style has had a major impact on the identification of Protohistoric archaeological remains in south-central Arizona. Notably, Di Peso (1953:148–154) also identified a red ware type, "Sobaipuri Red," but this type is largely restricted to the site of Quiburi and may represent Spanish influence on local pottery styles (Barnes 1984:218; Masse 1981:37–38); thus its identification has not had a major impact on Protohistoric studies.

Much of the published archaeological evidence for the Protohistoric derives from the Tucson Basin and surrounding zones in southern Arizona and consists of single-phase sites and features forming parts of multiple-component sites (see Seymour 1989, 1993, 1997; Whittlesey 1996). Most inferences have been based on identifications of Sobaipuri Plain and Whetstone Plain pottery. For example, Doelle (1984:197–200) lists 10 instances in which "Sobaipuri pottery" or "Sobaipuri projectile points" were recovered from excavations in and around the Tucson Basin, noting that in each case the materials were intermixed with historic or prehistoric remains (Ayres 1971; Brew and Huckell 1987; Huckell 1980, 1984; Huckell 1981; Simpson and Wells 1983).

Ravesloot and Whittlesey (1987) discuss the evidence from several additional sites in the region, including Second Canyon Ruin (Franklin 1980), Alder Wash Ruin (Masse 1981), England Ranch Ruin (Doyel 1977), the Tinaja Canyon site (Doyel 1977), and the San Xavier Bridge site (Ravesloot 1987), along with deposits in the Avra Valley (Dart 1994; Downum et al. 1986), the Santa Rita Mountains (Huckell 1984), and the Picacho Mountains (Wallace and Holmlund 1986). Many of these sites have oval, rock-ringed houses similar to those at Gaybanipitea (see Di Peso 1953:62), and many have thin, plain, brown ware ceramic assemblages (see Cable 1990:23.57–23.65). It is important to point out, however, that many of these inferred Protohistoric sites probably date to early Historic times, from about 1700 to 1850.

Two other studies, not included in the list above, are worth mentioning. The first is the Hecla Mine study by Goodyear (1977), which examined the archaeological evidence, composed principally of ceramic sherds, for Protohistoric occupation of the Slate Mountains region in the Santa Rosa Valley. One of the distinctive pottery types Goodyear describes is a thin, hand-wiped brown ware, which he originally compared to the Yuman "Tizon Brownware" tradition (Dobyns and Euler 1958). Subsequent studies, however, determined that the pottery more closely resembles Whetstone Plain, as reported by Di Peso (1953:154–156) and the thin brown ware correlate reported by Haury (1950:345). The second study of interest is a survey of the Santa Cruz Valley by Downum (1993), who recognizes as many as 14 sites as Protohistoric based on the presence of ceramics resembling Whetstone Plain ware. Many of these sites represent multiple-component settlements, however, where artifact assemblages often were found to be mixed with those from other time periods. Thus, it is uncertain if all of the sites represent Protohistoric occupations.

Inferred Protohistoric remains from the Phoenix Basin are less numerous. This is probably because Protohistoric materials often are mixed among prehistoric and historic occupations, making their identification in the field difficult or impossible. In addition, if the Spanish texts accurately describe early historic settlement patterns in the Phoenix Basin, then the paucity of identifiable remains may reflect the lack of large villages, since populations in this area appear to have been highly dispersed among small *rancherías*. For example, work in the Ak-Chin Indian Community in the southwestern portion of the Phoenix Basin has revealed 14 inferred Protohistoric or early Historic sites, 12 of which consist of *ranchería* settlements located at the end of an alluvial fan, where floodwater farming would have been possible (Gasser 1990:21–23).

At Ak-Chin, between 20 and 25 structures may have been present at the Painted Horse/Frog Pot settlement complex, while as many as 40 structures (not all contemporaneously occupied) composed the Whimsy Flat complex (Masse 1990). Many of these structures could represent short-term camps, however. The structures often were identified as "irregular patches of burned and ashy soil with charcoal flecking within an oval or circular outline" found just below the present ground surface without plastered floors or plastered hearths (Macnider and Gasser 1990:11.15). Most features measure between 2 m and 4 m in diameter and have associated postholes and shallow, basin-shaped hearths or fire-pits. Much of this occupation appears to post-date A.D. 1700 (Masse 1990:12.36), however, and should be considered early Historic.

More recently, one *ranchería*-style settlement has been partially excavated at Pueblo Salado along the Salt River in the central Phoenix Basin. Here, Wenker et al. (1996) discuss an oval-shaped pit house with three hearth features, archaeomagnetically dated between A.D. 1375 and 1750, and a canal segment that yielded a calibrated radiocarbon date between A.D. 1443 and 1955. In adjacent features, the authors recovered Protohistoric ceramics, namely, Jeddito Black-on-yellow (dated to about A.D. 1300 to 1600/1625; Adams et al. 1993; Colton 1956; Windes 1977), and Pima Plain, Pima Red, and Pima Red-on-buff (all dating to about A.D. 1400 to 1840; Douglas 1953; Drucker 1941; Hayden 1959).

CHAPTER 2

MAJOR CHALLENGES IN
PROTOHISTORIC RESEARCH

The past 20 years have witnessed a steady increase in the number of features, deposits, and materials inferred to date to Protohistoric times in southern Arizona. This is partly the result of the increased pace of cultural resource mitigation work completed in the region, which has uncovered new occupations in modern metropolitan areas. Still, many small Protohistoric settlements may never be identified and investigated, since they are not always eligible for inclusion in the National Register of Historic Places, and so are not mitigated at the same level of intensity as many large sites with long occupation spans. This is partly because the material assemblages associated with these sites are generally ephemeral and sparse, and partly due to the failure of researchers to perceive the information potential of these kinds of sites. Nevertheless, accurate temporal placement and site and feature identification remain the two most critical challenges to archaeological research on the Protohistoric period. In this section, I discuss each of these issues, pointing out some of their evidential constraints.

DATING THE PROTOHISTORIC

The overview presented in Chapter 1 indicates that our understanding of the temporal components of the Protohistoric period is poor. Improving chronology is a problem with broad significance, with important implications for modeling the timing and pace of reorganization of Hohokam society at the end of the Classic period. In addition, chronological resolution for the Protohistoric can provide crucial information for better understanding the temporal aspects of Spanish contact and, by extension, some of the social and ecological factors that conditioned interactions between indigenous populations and Europeans.

Currently, very few absolute chronometric dates are available from inferred post-Classic sites in southern Arizona. Table 2 lists the published radiocarbon dates for these sites. The dates range broadly from A.D. 1277 to A.D. 1859, and in some cases different samples from the same specimen have produced multiple dates or date ranges (e.g., Ravesloot and Whittlesey 1987; Zyniecki 1993). In viewing these data, however, it is clear that most dates derive from late Classic/early post-Classic occupations, with relatively few from later sites. Further, it may be significant that all dated materials from the earlier part of the period (i.e., Polvorón phase) derive from the Phoenix Basin, while most dated materials from early Historic sites come from the Tucson Basin. The circumscribed distribution of the late Classic/early post-Classic sites suggests that Polvorón phase settlement, if it is indeed distinct from Classic occupations, may have been a regional phenomenon restricted to the Phoenix Basin. Ultimately, these observations signal the need for more excavation in the greater Phoenix Basin with the specific objective of locating and studying potential Protohistoric settlements.

Table 2. Radiocarbon Dates from Protohistoric Sites in South-central Arizona.

Site	Calibrated C-14 Range[a]	Material	Context	Reference
Ak-Chin site	AD 1709-1859	wood charcoal	house fill	Gasser et al. 1990
AZ AA:12:131	AD 1650-1720	wood charcoal	roasting pit	Ravesloot and Whittlesey 1987:Table 7.4
AZ BB:13:14	AD 1460-1800	wood charcoal	roasting pit	Ravesloot and Whittlesey 1987:Table 7.4
AZ BB:13:14	AD 1530-1810	wood charcoal	fire pit on structure floor	Ravesloot and Whittlesey 1987:Table 7.4
AZ BB:13:14	AD 1650-1810	wood charcoal	roasting pit	Ravesloot and Whittlesey 1987:Table 7.4
AZ DD:8:129	AD 1680-1740?	wood charcoal	roasting pit	Ravesloot and Whittlesey 1987:Table 7.4
Dutch Canal Ruin	AD 1277-1405	wood charcoal	extramural pit (Feature 8-14)	Greenwald and Ballagh 1993
Dutch Canal Ruin	AD 1280-1405	wood charcoal	fire pit on structure floor (Feature 8-3-1)	Greenwald and Ballagh 1993
Dutch Canal Ruin	AD 1284-1405	wood charcoal	extramural pit (Feature 8-14)	Greenwald and Ballagh 1993
Dutch Canal Ruin	AD 1284-1423	wood charcoal	extramural pit (Feature 8-12)	Greenwald and Ballagh 1993
Dutch Canal Ruin	AD 1292-1405	wood charcoal	fire pit on structure floor (Feature 8-3-1)	Greenwald and Ballagh 1993
Dutch Canal Ruin	AD 1302-1431	wood charcoal	extramural pit (Feature 8-12)	Greenwald and Ballagh 1993
El Polvorón	AD 1441-1635	wood charcoal	architectural element	Sires 1984:301; Dean 1991:130
Grand Canal Ruins, AZ:T:12:14	AD 1295-1403	wood charcoal	cremation	Mitchell 1989
Grand Canal Ruins, AZ:T:12:14	AD 1310-1433	wood charcoal	unknown feature	Mitchell 1989
Grand Canal Ruins, AZ:T:12:14	AD 1310-1449	wood charcoal	cremation	Mitchell 1989
Grand Canal Ruins, AZ:T:12:14	AD 1430-1473	wood charcoal	pit house	Mitchell 1989
Grand Canal Ruins, AZ:T:12:16	AD 1283-1391	wood charcoal	inhumation	Mitchell 1989
Los Guanacos	AD 1414-1445	wood charcoal	structure fill	Howell 1993:145
Pueblo Salado	AD 1415-1640	wood charcoal	roasting pit	Greenwald et al. 1996:508
Pueblo Salado	AD 1425-1650	wood charcoal	roasting pit	Greenwald et al. 1996:507

[a] one sigma range reported

The broad range of dates in Table 2 may simply reflect a methodological constraint of radiocarbon dating, since this technique reaches its upper limit of sensitivity after the A.D. 1500s (Dean 1991:96; Doyel 1995:485–486; Ravesloot and Whittlesey 1987:96–97). A similar problem applies to archaeomagnetic dating (Wolfman 1984; e.g., Deaver 1989; Eighmy and Doyel 1987; Eighmy and Hathaway 1987; Eighmy and McGuire 1989). One potentially useful alternative to these techniques is thermoluminescence (TL) dating of ceramic materials, since this procedure is not subject to the calibration problems that prevent radiocarbon and archaeomagnetic dating from providing reasonably modest intervals for sites occurring after the 1500s (Feathers 1997; e.g., Crown and Sires 1984; Dykeman et al. 2002; Feathers 2000; Rice 1998b). Further, TL dating provides temporal information for cultural products rather than natural ones—a potentially important difference given the sparse nature of Protohistoric assemblages with organic remains.

However, there are two important limitations to TL dating of ceramic materials. First, unlike radiocarbon dating, which dates one of the growth rings from a tree before it was cut down, TL dating reveals the date of the combustion event associated with firing pottery and not of the feature or deposit with which the ceramic is associated. This may be a problem in cases where pottery is traded or curated over long periods. Second, while the intervals produced from TL dating are generally shorter and sometimes more reliable than radiocarbon or archaeomagnetic dating, variation in testing parameters, particularly archaeological dose (accumulated radiation) and anomalous fading (loss of a normally stable signal through time), often make it difficult to fit the specimen's decay to a logarithmic function, and thus to determine a corrected age for the sample.

For example, in his investigation of the Sweetwater site (GR-931) near the middle Gila River, Woodson (2002:214, 218; Woodson and Morgan 2002:120) used TL dating of a ceramic sherd (Sample UW734) to date a pottery manufacturing area to the late Classic or early post-Classic (corrected, A.D. 1456 ± 53), although Feathers (2002:274–275) notes that high radioactivity and anomalous fading resulted in a younger than expected date for the sample. Other specimens dated by TL from features in the same depositional stratum as Sample UW734 at Sweetwater produced dates ranging from A.D. 1658 ± 66 to 1836 ± 49, suggesting that the sample or its TL date may be problematic.

Apart from absolute dating, it has been argued that changes in the proportions of certain pottery wares in assemblages may signal at least the start of the Protohistoric. Over the course of the Classic period, the production of buff ware pottery appears to have decreased while the manufacture of red wares increased (Abbott 1994). Sires (1984:265–273), for example, suggests that the Polvorón phase is marked at El Polvorón by contrasting frequencies of buff ware and red ware. Compared to the ceramic collection from the Classic site of Las Colinas, Casa Grande Red-on-buff ceramics are found at El Polvorón in very low proportions, comprising just 0.03 percent of the entire collection. In contrast, at El Polvorón, red wares make up nearly 34 percent of the assemblage, while at Las Colinas they represent 18 percent of the collection during the Soho phase and slightly more (23.5 percent) during the Civano phase. It also may be significant that Sires (1984) notes particularly high numbers of red-on-brown ceramics, similar to those from the Tucson Basin, although some of these may have been manufactured locally (P. Crown, personal communication, 2003).

Sires (1984) and others (e.g., Chenault 1993, 1996, 2000) believe that these temporal shifts in ceramic proportions mark the end of Classic period traditions and may allow archaeologists to date initial post-Classic occupations at sites in the Phoenix Basin. Hackbarth (1995:178–179) points out, however, that differences in site size and function may account for the contrasting ceramic frequencies: Las Colinas is a large, multiple-component site with a complex depositional history located at the end of a large canal system, while El Polvorón is a smaller, single-phase farmstead located on a large wash. Additionally, these differences may simply represent unequal sampling between the sites; a much larger portion of El Polvorón was excavated relative to Las Colinas. Nevertheless, work at other sites in the Phoenix Basin that have late Classic or post-Classic assemblages has revealed similar patterns of low proportions of buff ware and high proportions of red ware (e.g., Abbott 1994; Howell 1993).

In addition to studying changes in the assemblage proportions of ceramic wares, it has been argued that the ratios of certain temper types associated with plain wares, such as phyllite, schist, and sand, are temporally sensitive (e.g., Abbott 1994; Cable and Gould 1988; Cable and Mitchell 1988; Crown 1981; Deaver 1990; Newman and Woodson 2002). Henderson (1995:106–109), for example, found shared technological characteristics in the late Classic and Historic assemblages at Pueblo Patricio in the central Phoenix Basin. She found plain ware sherds with fine-grained temper composed of "rolled [alluvial] mixed sands [with quartz and feldspar] bearing volcanic grains in a laminar or silty paste" (Henderson 1995:109; compare Beckwith 1986:61; Whittlesey 1986:86) in both assemblages. Crushed sherd tempers with similar pastes and physical attributes (carbon streaking, thick slips, dark red colors) also were present in both assemblages. Similar temper types associated with pottery from inferred Protohistoric deposits also have been noted at Pueblo Salado (Walsh-Anduze 1993, 1996a, 1996b). In the middle Gila survey collection, pottery with fine-grained rolled sand temper has been recovered from survey and excavation at Sweetwater (Woodson 2002:252) and the Blackwater site (Beckwith 1986:61; Whittlesey 1986:86).

These findings suggest that similar technologies were used in the manufacture of some types of prehistoric and historic pottery (see also Waugh 1995, 2002; Whittlesey 1997a). As such, there may be some degree of continuity between technological practices that developed during the late Classic period and ceramic traditions of historic potters. Henderson (1995:110) suggests that, "If a common pottery tradition is expressed in the late prehistoric and historic eras, then it seems likely that the tradition would also be represented in the Protohistoric era." It is important to point out, however, that these patterns may be specific to the central Phoenix Basin, since it has been demonstrated that potters in this area tended to use temper that was immediately available to them in particular "sand-composition zones" (Abbott 1994:145).

IDENTIFYING THE PROTOHISTORIC

The studies discussed above indicate that both absolute and relative dating techniques are useful for resolving chronological issues in Protohistoric research. However, before these analyses can be applied to Protohistoric studies, more effective methods need to be developed for detecting appropriate archaeological features for chronological study as well as ceramic and flaked stone assemblages for stylistic and technological seriations. Table 3 provides a summary of inferred Protohistoric sites and features by type in south-central Arizona, based on published literature. The relatively low numbers of reported sites and features may reflect the fact that many sites have been destroyed by agricultural development and subsequent urban expansion in the Phoenix and Tucson basins. Another problem, however, is that there are very few diagnostic criteria on which to draw for recognizing Protohistoric remains and distinguishing them from Classic period material culture. This point deserves greater attention, because if we are going to make any progress in identifying Protohistoric occupations, then we need to focus more energy on developing ways to recognize and evaluate some of the diagnostic material traits of the period.

At present, the evidence cited most often to infer the presence of Protohistoric sites and deposits is restricted to "Sobaipuri" projectile points and pottery, although the presence of unifaces also has been suggested to be an important characteristic (Brew and Huckell 1987; Masse 1981). Describing "Sonoran" points in the mid-1700s, Pfefferkorn (1989) states, "This [triangular pointed flint] is about one inch long, not quite an inch wide, and as thick in the middle as the back of a strong knife. The edges, however, are filed as thin as a single card and are armed all along with sharp saw teeth." Serrated points with deeply concave bases also appear to be common at late sites along the San Pedro River (e.g., Di Peso 1951, 1953; Justice 2002; Masse 1981), which is the location generally associated with the Sobaipuri.

These materials, however, have been the subjects of intense debate. Some archaeologists disagree with Masse's (1981:39) and others' (e.g., Brew and Huckell 1987; Doelle 1984; Justice 2002:272; see also Haury 1950, 1976; Rosenthal et al. 1978) identification of "Sobaipuri" projectile points—small, triangular, concave-based points with finely serrated edges that were first identified at Quiburi (Di Peso 1951). For example, Ravesloot and Whittlesey (1987:94–96) note that the manufacture of points recovered from each site appears to have been standardized (their shapes and sizes do not vary significantly), suggesting that they were crafted by relatively few individuals (see also Whittaker 1984). In addition, they argue that, given no concrete contextual or independent chronometric evidence to support the classification of these points as Sobaipuri, their identification as such is unwarranted (see also Euler 1987).

In their detailed study of projectile points recovered from Historic period villages along the middle Gila, Loendorf and Rice (2004:58–62) identify two types of points that may have been manufactured in Protohistoric times. One type ("Straight Base Triangular," thought to be associated with the Pima) consists of small triangular points that lack notching or a stem and have straight to slightly concave bases. A second type ("U-shaped Base Triangular," thought to be associated with the Sobaipuri) also lacks notching or a stem, but has moderately to deeply concave bases. Separating these two types using basal concavity is problematic, however, because this variable appears to have a continuous rather than modal distribution. They find that attribute data for both point types vary along a continuum such that the two styles represent extremes of that range. The data suggest to them that much of the variation in point attributes is local to individual sites. As a result, inferring Protohistoric occupations based solely on the presence of projectile point styles is problematic.

Table 3. Summary of Published Protohistoric Sites and Features in South–central Arizona.

Occupation Type	Salt-Gila Basin		San Pedro Valley		Santa Cruz Valley		Totals
	n	%[a]	n	%	n	%	
Sites							
Village	3	12	6	23	17	65	26
Ranchería	19	70			8	30	27
Terrace Site					6	100	6
Rockshelter					2	100	2
Campsite					6	100	6
Petroglyph Site					1	100	1
House			7	47	8	53	15
Subtotals	22	27	13	16	48	58	83
Features							
Artifact Scatter	43	81			10	19	53
Agricultural Field					2	100	2
Roasting Pit			6	86	1	14	7
Canal	1	100					1
Well	1	100					1
Burial					5	100	5
Subtotals	45	65	6	9	18	26	69
Totals	67	44	19	13	66	43	152

[a] row percent

With regards to "Sobaipuri pottery," Masse (1981:37–38) questions some of Di Peso's (1953) original claims regarding the cultural affiliation of Sobaipuri Plain pottery. Masse argues that Whetstone Plain was the pottery type most likely associated with the Protohistoric Sobaipuri, and not Sobaipuri Plain, which he believes represents early historic ceramics manufactured by Tohono O'odham or Opata groups. Subsequently, Ravesloot and Whittlesey (1987) have noted several problems surrounding Masse's equation of Whetstone Plain with the Sobaipuri. One major issue is the lack of technical studies and descriptions of Sobaipuri material culture. Existing descriptions of Whetstone Plain and Sobaipuri Plain, for example, are "internally variable and display attributes at variance from Di Peso's original type description" (Ravesloot and Whittlesey 1987:93; e.g., Waugh 1995). Clearly, more detailed technological studies and attribute analyses of Sobaipuri Plain and Whetstone Plain from regional collections are required to resolve these issues. Imperative to these studies are similar analyses of late Classic and early Historic plain ware pottery with which to develop a comparative sample for deriving testable implications for Protohistoric plain wares (e.g.,

Abbott 1994; Deaver 1990; Henderson 1995; Waugh 2002; Whittlesey 1982, 1997a). The assemblages from three Historic sites along the middle Gila, in particular, may prove important in this regard: Alicia (Rice et al. 1983), Blackwater (Layhe 1986), and Sweetwater (Woodson, ed. 2002).

The presence of other ceramic types, apart from Sobaipuri wares, sometimes are cited to infer Protohistoric occupations, such as Pima Plain, Pima Red, and Pima Red-on-buff, dated between A.D. 1400 and 1850 (see descriptions in Douglas 1953; Drucker 1941; Fontana et al. 1962:116–117; Haury 1976; Hayden 1959; Hrdlička 1906:43–44; Kisselburg 1989; Layhe 1986; Russell 1908:124–131; Shenk and Teague 1975:60–61; Wood 1987:114). In their study of historic and modern Papago pottery, Fontana and colleagues (1962:103–105; see also Haury et al. 1950:344–345) describe two variants of "Papago Plain," an indigenous plain ware suspected to derive from early Spanish contact sites (from about A.D. 1700 to 1860). Variant 1 is described as hand-smoothed bowls or jars with medium to thick walls with rim coils. Variant 2 is represented by highly polished bowls with thin walls without rim coils. They also note the presence of Papago Red-on-brown (Haury et al. 1950:350), Papago Glaze (Caywood 1950), Papago White-on-red or Brown (Haury et al. 1950:350), and Papago Red (Haury et al. 1950:346–347; Scantling 1940:30–32) at early Spanish contact sites. These types have not been studied very thoroughly, however, and a high degree of intra-site variation could make regional identifications of ceramic patterns difficult. As such, these wares do not represent a reliable means for identifying Protohistoric sites at present.

Recently, however, the excavation of two early Historic sites in the western portion of the middle Gila River Valley—Whimsy Flat (AZ T:16:71 [ASM]) and Frog Pot (AZ T:16:23 [ASM])—produced relatively large collections of pottery that may be useful for identifying Protohistoric assemblages (Deaver 1990:15.11–15.19). Ceramics at Whimsy Flat represent four types of plain wares (Buff Plain, Micaceous Plain, Coarse Sand-tempered Plain, and Crushed Schist Plain), along with low frequencies of Red-on-buff. Generally, the plain wares are thin walled, averaging 4 mm in thickness, with well-smoothed and even surfaces. Most surfaces are hand-wiped, but anvil marks are still present on some jar interiors, indicating a coil/paddle-and-anvil construction technique. Forms include bowls and jars, each with either direct (straight) or slightly everted (flared) rims.

Ceramics at Frog Pot are similar to those at Whimsy Flat, but also contain some bowl and jar sherds that have folded rims and show evidence of a clay stucco applied to their exteriors; nearly 1.5 percent of the Buff Plain and 35 percent of the Micaceous Plain have stuccoed exteriors. The clay stucco was only applied to the lower half of vessels, as evidenced on two reconstructable pots. Deaver (1990:15.12) speculates, based on the form and finish of vessels in the assemblage, that Buff Plain pots were used as water jars, storage jars, and serving dishes. In contrast, he (Deaver 1990:15.14) proposes that Micaceous Plain and Coarse Sand-tempered Plain vessels probably represent cooking pots similar to Papago Bean pots (Fontana et al. 1962) and Patayan III cooking pots (Waters 1982).

Deaver (1990:15.17) observes that the pottery from Whimsy Flat and Frog Pot shares few technological characteristics with later historic pottery from the region or historic Papago pottery (Bruder 1975; Fontana et al. 1962; Teague 1980). Instead, he believes that there are strong similarities between the middle Gila assemblages and those of the Lowland Patayan of the Lower Colorado. For example, the folded rim and clay stucco attributes that appear in the Frog Pot collections also appear in Patayan III pottery (Patayan Palomas Buff; Rogers 1936; Waters 1982; Withers 1941), but not in historic Pima pottery (see Fontana et al. 1962). More recently, however, Newman and Woodson (2002:163–166) report clay stucco surface treatment and folded rims on early Historic buff and plain ware pottery from the Sweetwater site in the middle Gila Valley (GR-931). In addition, exterior coatings of clay stucco have been observed on Classic period Hohokam pots at Snaketown in the middle Gila region (Haury 1976:225) and in the Tucson Basin (Heidke and Elson 1988). Di Peso (1956:299) also reported stucco on reconstructible vessels and sherds of Ramanote Plain recovered from his excavations at Paloparado, which may date to Protohistoric or early Historic times (however a reassessment by Wilcox [1987] suggests the site dates to the Classic period). These technological similarities between pottery in the Lower Colorado River and southern Arizona suggest a close interrelationship between Piman groups and some Yuman tribes that probably extended into prehistoric times (e.g., Cable 1990; Doelle and Wallace 1987).

Along with the descriptions of early Historic pottery from Whimsy Flat and Frog Pot, certain ceramic types with established manufacturing dates produced elsewhere in the Southwest but found in settlements in central Arizona can be useful for inferring the Protohistoric in the middle Gila basin (e.g., Bayman and Ryan 1988; Betancourt 1978:60–61; Crown 1983, 1984; Deaver 1990). These include Jeddito Black-on-yellow (A.D. 1300 to 1600/1625; Adams et al. 1993; Colton 1956; Windes 1977) from the Hopi region and Matsaki polychrome (A.D. 1400 to 1680; Colton 1958; Fowler 1989; Kintigh 1985) from the Zuni area. Intrusive ceramics such as these, however, are generally rare and thus do not offer a consistent means for inferring Protohistoric occupations.

Together, these observations suggest that the Protohistoric period may be inferred from multiple lines of evidence from independent data sets, mainly those based on studies of pottery and projectile points. However, much of this information necessarily derives from excavation. In contrast, there are very few studies that make use of archaeological survey data for inferring Protohistoric settlement. One of the challenges in identifying the Protohistoric, then, is to develop new methods for evaluating survey data. This is especially important for the middle Gila survey because most of our data represent surface collections.

CHAPTER 3

THE PROTOHISTORIC OCCUPATION
OF THE MIDDLE GILA RIVER VALLEY

Little is known about the middle Gila region during the sixteenth and seventeenth centuries from Spanish reports, and even less is known from archaeological evidence. The first step to identifying evidence for Protohistoric occupation is to identify potential candidates for study. In this section, I examine Spanish reports, historical information, and archaeological evidence to identify possible areas of Protohistoric occupation along the middle Gila.

SPANISH REPORTS

Father Eusebio Kino's journey to the Gila River Pimas and the Casa Grande ruin in 1694 was the first recorded visit by a European to the middle Gila River Valley, although he had previously traveled from his mission at Dolores in northern Sonora as far north as Tumacácori in 1691 and to San Xavier del Bac in 1692 (Bolton 1919:118–129). These were not the first visits by Spaniards to southern Arizona, however, and earlier records make reference to the native peoples in the sixteenth and early seventeenth centuries. One reference comes from Francisco de Vásquez de Coronado when his expedition to Cibola crossed Sonora and southern Arizona in 1540–1542. He reported that his expedition passed through peoples of the same language as far as the wilderness of Chichilticale (Hammond and Rey 1940:250). Chichilticale (also spelled "Chichilticalli," meaning "red house" in Nahuatl), was probably one of the pueblo ruins of southeastern Arizona built in the late A.D. 1200s or 1300s and abandoned around 1400 (Duffen and Hartmann 1997; Haury 1984; Sauer 1932). To reach the wilderness of Chichilticale, Coronado's army traversed a broad region populated by Pimas, all speaking closely related languages or dialects (Wilson 1999:1.6–1.7). In his report to Viceroy Mendoza, sent from Cibola, August 3, 1540, Coronado (Hammond and Rey 1940:41–42) writes:

> when I reached Chichilticale I found that I was fifteen days' journey distant from the sea. . . . The Indians of Chichilticale say that when they go to the sea for fish, or for anything else that they need, they go across the country, and that it takes them ten days; and this information which I have received from the Indians appears to me to be true.
>
> I rested for two days at Chichilticale, and there was good reason for staying longer, because we found that the horses were becoming so tired; but there was no chance to rest longer, because the food was giving out. I entered the borders of the wilderness region on Saint

John's eve, and, for a change from our past labors, we found no grass during the first days, but a worse way through mountains and more dangerous passages than we had experienced previously.

. . . the way is very bad for at least 30 leagues and more, through impassable mountains. But when we had passed these 30 leagues, we found fresh rivers and grass like that of Castile, and especially one sort like what we call Scaramoio; many nut and mulberry trees, but the leaves of the nut trees are different from those of Spain. There was a considerable amount of flax near the banks of one river, which was called on this account El Rio del Lino.

Around this time, Captain Hernando de Alarçon sailed to the head of the Gulf of California with his three ships bearing supplies for Coronado. This mission continued up the Colorado River and, although Alarçon claimed to have voyaged upstream for 85 leagues, he did not mention the mouth of the Gila River, which later diarists placed 20 to 30 leagues from the gulf (Dunne 1955:25; Ezell 1963:61–65; Hammond and Rey 1940:124–155; Harwell and Kelly 1983:84). Although Captain Alarçon had nothing to say about the Gila River area or its residents, Coronado's chroniclers found the context for local relationships much the same in the country they traversed, which they called *tierra guerra*, "warring country" (Hammond and Rey 1940:251, 269). According to Wilson (1999:1.8), "The Southwest in 1540 was not a peaceful place, and local wars that were launched simply for their own sakes probably had much to do with changes in the cultural geography and causing some areas to be without settled populations."

Another reference to the populations living in the vicinity of the middle Gila comes from Fray Gerónimo de Zárate Salmerón, a missionary based in New Mexico from 1621 until 1626 (Milich 1966; see also Wilson 1999:1.8–1.9). According to Zárate Salmerón, the *rio del nombre de Jesús* (Gila River) flowed between barren mountains, from southeast to northwest. The entire river appears to have been settled by the "Ozara" (also spelled Ocara, Osera, and Oseca) Indians, and their multitude was very great. They drew signs on the ground of 20 *rancherías* or *pueblos* (Milich 1966:71). From this account, it appears that Piman-speaking peoples lived in southern Arizona during the sixteenth and early seventeenth centuries, but they had not yet differentiated into the named groups known from a century later. The inhabitants of the lower Gila River in 1605 were probably exclusively Pimans, as were those who made their homes in the San Pedro and perhaps also the Santa Cruz river valleys (Wilson 1999:1.9). It is not known, however, whether anyone at this time dwelt along the middle Gila River.

HISTORICAL INFORMATION

At least four major villages, each represented by multiple communities or settlement districts, were established near the banks of the middle Gila River by the early nineteenth century; one in the vicinity of Sacaton, another at Sweetwater, a third at Casa Blanca, and one near Pima Butte (Figure 4). Survey data indicate that these settlements may have been

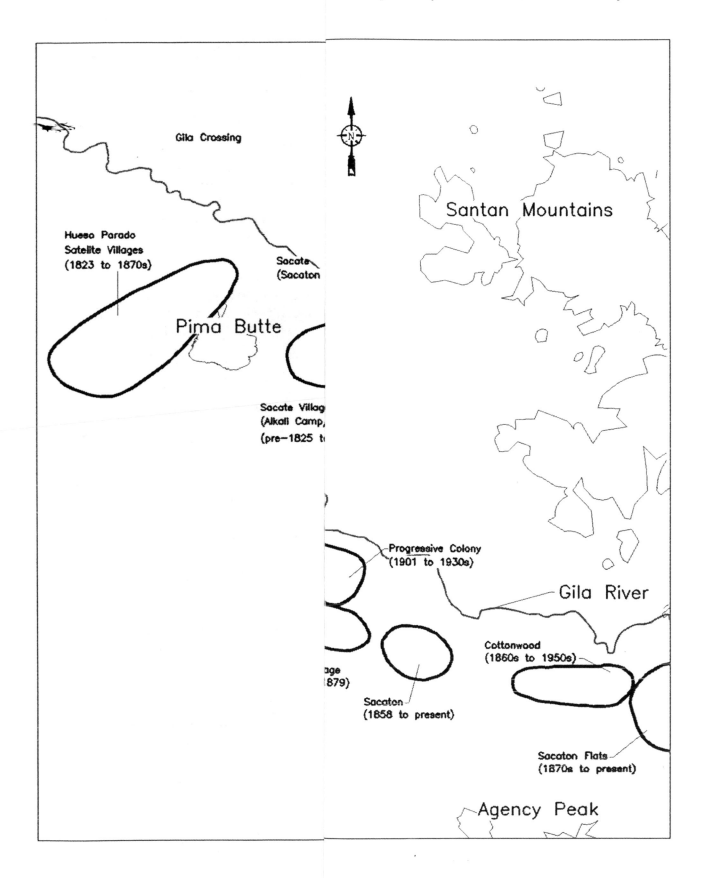

Gila Crossing

Hueso Parado
Satelite Villages
(1823 to 1870s)

Socate
(Sacaton

Pima Butte

Socate Villag
(Alkali Camp,
(pre–1825 t

Santan Mountains

Progressive Colony
(1901 to 1930s)

Gila River

Cottonwood
(1860s to 1950s)

age
879)

Sacaton
(1858 to present)

Sacaton Flats
(1870s to present)

Agency Peak

established on the remains of Protohistoric occupations (Eiselt et al. 2002:639–645). In the 1850s, Pima villages, such as those along the middle Gila, were composed of several related families and were populated by 200 to as many as 600 individuals representing up to 50 *rancherías* (Ezell 1961). In addition to *rancherías*, villages also included cemeteries, agricultural fields, irrigation ditches or canals associated with temporary camps, and loosely defined resource procurement areas, such as hunting catchments and wells (Wilson 1999). Village administration included headmen and a council of elders who acted both at the village and regional levels (Ezell 1961:124–127). Each settlement district appears to have maintained a "council house" or "socio-ceremonial house," a communal building that functioned as a meeting place and a space for conducting ceremonies (Ezell 1961:128–130; Russell 1908:155), perhaps similar to the "reception houses" among groups in southern Arizona described by Bernal (Smith 1966:45), Kino (Smith 1966:27), and Manje (Burrus 1971:202–205; Karns 1954:80–89, 125) in the late 1690s.

The Sacaton district represents a relatively late historic occupation brought about primarily through the establishment of several Euroamerican facilities in the 1850s, including a Butterfield stage stop, a trading store, an agency, and several schools and churches built by C. H. Cook. The O'odham did not inhabit the area prior to 1850 to a great extent, although there are some indications that a village called Tusonimo or La Encarnación may have been located in the vicinity in the 1700s. Apache raiding probably was the cause for abandonment of this area as well as for a general constriction of O'odham territory by the mid-1700s (Winter 1973). Apache raiding likely restricted most settlement to the south bank of the Gila River, in open places nearer to Casa Blanca and Sweetwater from the late 1700s until 1870. The Pee Posh village of Hol-che-dum (GR-888 and possibly GR-921) originated a few miles east of O'odham territory in the Sacaton district by the 1840s. This settlement is likely the earliest late Historic village in the district, which was largely abandoned by the 1870s. Villagers in the Sacaton district after 1870 moved to the area from many different places, including Old Mount Top, Hol-che-dum, and the Santa Rosa Mountains. Many of the Old Santan villagers moved to the north side of the river in 1879, and many of the original Pee Posh villagers moved out to Gila Crossing after the 1870s. With the establishment of Sacaton as a commercial and administrative center by the 1870s, O'odham occupation of the area increased dramatically.

The Sweetwater district is characterized by several large villages with long occupation spans, which experienced a general population decline throughout the late 1800s (see Woodson, ed. 2002). Early Spanish chroniclers consistently mention "Uturituc" as a large village in this area, and Southworth (1914) shows the phonetically similar "Old Hirchirlagairk Village" in roughly the same location. By the early 1800s, the focus of occupation may have shifted to Buen Llano (Stotonick), which was located in the vicinity of Rattlesnakes House or "Pimo Lookout," (GR-782)—a signaling station and lookout during the 1850s. The timing of this settlement shift may coincide with the development of O'odham tribal and military alliances from 1697 to 1846 (Winter 1973:74). Materials from this site and areas surrounding it (e.g., GR-931 and GR-886) probably date to the 1800s, although occupation may date as early as the late 1700s. Evidence for the modern Sweetwater Village appears by the late 1800s (Woodson, ed. 2002). This village was established north of Old Hirchirlagairk in the vicinity of GR-931, and modern occupations are present there today. A general pattern of population decline in the Sweetwater district began in the 1860s, with people moving to the Sacaton district, Blackwater, and other areas off the reservation.

The Casa Blanca district is composed of the historic and modern portions of Casa Blanca, the Bapchule community, and two short-lived satellite communities to the north. As at Sweetwater, the Casa Blanca district witnessed a significant population influx due to Apache raiding. Several small villages were relocated closer to Casa Blanca during the 1800s, but then moved away once the Apaches were placed on a reservation. Population levels grew throughout the nineteenth and twentieth centuries due to the establishment of Casa Blanca as an administrative and commercial center by 1850. Wilson (1999) suggests that Casa Blanca was the location of Tubus Cabors, which was established during the 1770s. By the early 1800s, the same village is called La Tierra Amontonada, and by the early 1900s, it is known as Vahki or "Wakey." A 1937 map of the area by R. A. Dupont shows Old Vahki, New Vahki, and Casa Blanca, suggesting that the settlement changed locations over time. Finally, Sratuka and Wet Camp are communities to the north of Casa Blanca. Sratuka (GR-497 and GR-498) was the first to be established on the south side of the river, with villagers farming the north side during the years of Apache raiding. When floods destroyed this village in 1872, many of these people dispersed to the Salt River or to Snaketown on the north bank of the Gila. Others moved closer to Casa Blanca to form Wet Camp.

Current survey does not include much of the archaeological material present in the Sacate district, although current work is underway at several large village locations. These include GR-909 (the Sacate Village) and GR-935 (Old Sranuka). Initial survey results demonstrate a continuous and dense distribution of historic materials that extend from Pima Butte to Sratuka. Sacate Village may include the remains of the 1700s village, Sudaccson or Sutaquissón, but it also encompasses nineteenth and twentieth century occupations associated with Alkali Camp or Sranuka. Areas to the east of Sacate Village probably encompass the old village of Sranuka, which was located closer to Casa Blanca during the height of Apache raiding from the 1840s to the 1880s. This area was abandoned after the cessation of the Apache raids, and the village was reestablished at Pima Butte some time after 1880. The Sacate district also probably includes a mixture of O'odham and Pee Posh materials. The early 1800s Pee Posh village of Hueso Parado probably was located at Maricopa Wells by 1825, and several smaller Pee Posh hamlets probably extended to Pima Butte; GR-1139 may represent one of these settlements. Many of the Hueso Parado Pee Posh moved to Gila Crossing when the sloughs and ponds of Maricopa Wells dried after 1870, but several others moved to areas surrounding Sacaton Station and Sacate Village.

ARCHAEOLOGICAL EVIDENCE

While the historic record of the middle Gila indicates several places to look for Protohistoric materials, the distribution of certain artifact types provides important clues to narrow the search. As Doelle (1984:197–200) and others (e.g., Di Peso 1951, 1953; Masse 1981:39; Ravesloot and Whittlesey 1987:94–96) have noted for sites in the Tucson Basin,

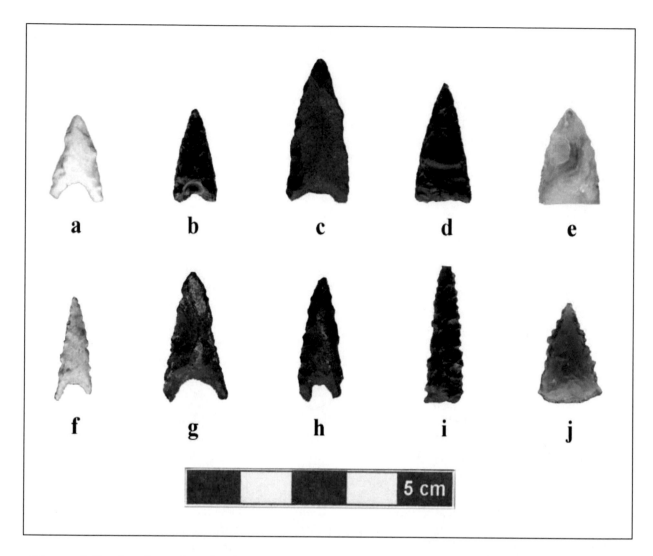

Figure 5. Projectile points from sites GR-909 and GR-1139 near the middle Gila River (after Loendorf and Rice 2004:Figure 8). Examples A, B, F, G, and H are U-shaped Base Triangular points; specimens D, E, I, and J are Straight Base Triangular points.

early Historic and Protohistoric sites have been inferred based on the presence of "Sobaipuri" projectile points, triangular concave-based points with serrated edges. Recently, Loendorf and Rice (2004:60–62) have studied attribute variability among points collected from middle Gila sites that are similar to Sobaipuri points, and have concluded that similar "O'odham points" were manufactured or used at some middle Gila sites between A.D. 1300 and 1950 (Figure 5). Indeed, these types of points are somewhat common in the middle Gila surface collection, representing roughly one quarter (n = 204) of the sample.

Further, Crown (1983, 1984; see also Hayden 1957:129) notes that proto-Hopi yellow wares, manufactured from about A.D. 1300 to 1600/1625 (Adams et al. 1993; Colton 1956; Windes 1977) were recovered from some of the post-Classic features at La Colinas, as at El Polvorón and many other inferred Polvorón phase sites. Hopi yellow wares also have been identified at several middle Gila sites (Figure 6). Thus, the presence of O'odham projectile

Figure 6. Examples of Hopi yellow ware sherds in the middle Gila survey collection. The uppermost specimen is from GR-1157, near Snaketown. The middle row includes (from left to right) sherds from GR-1139, GR-909, and GR-1157. The lowest row shows (from left to right) examples from GR-1139, GR-494, and GR-1164.

points and Hopi yellow wares among the historic middle Gila sites discussed above provides a means for identifying sites that may contain evidence for Protohistoric occupation.

Figure 7 shows the distribution of O'odham projectile points and Hopi yellow wares among middle Gila sites. The distribution of these artifacts is wide ranging, although it is notable that many are found in sites just south of the Gila River in the Casa Blanca district. Two of these sites (GR-909 and GR-1139) are of particular interest, because they represent significant Historic period villages (see Eiselt et al. 2002:95–98). Located close to the Gila River, Site GR-909 is the Akimel O'odham village of Sacate (including the settlements of Alkali Camp and Sranuka), which may include the ruins of Sudaccson (Sutaquissón), an

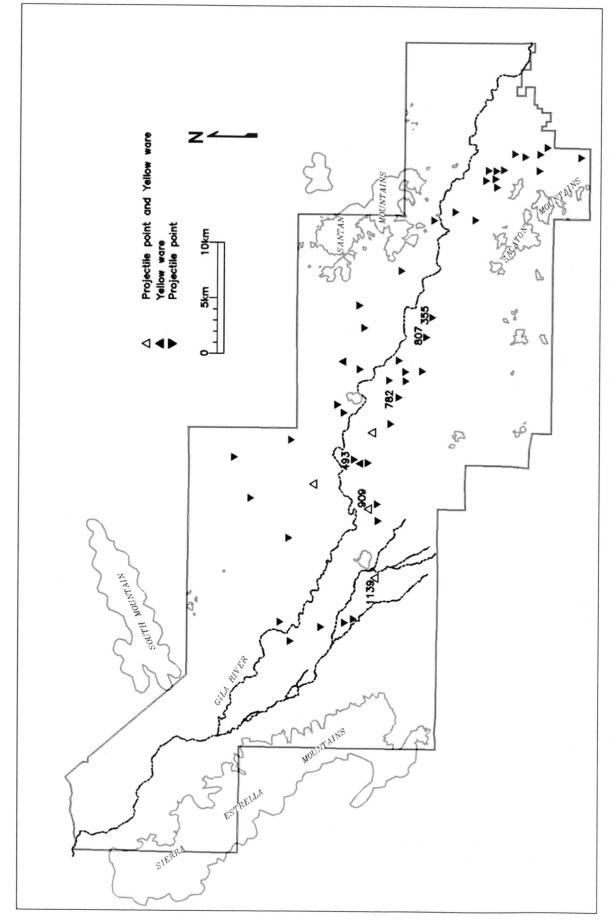

Figure 7. Distribution of proto-Hopi yellow wares and O-odham projectile points among archaeological sites on the Gila River Indian Community.

eighteenth-century village reported by Kino and Manje (Wilson 1999:2.5, 3.8; see also Bolton 1930; Ezell 1963). Recent settlement survey at Sacate shows that the site was occupied from as early as A.D. 1750 until 1850 (Darling et al. 2004; Randolph et al. 2002). Located roughly 3 km west of Sacate, Site GR-1139 sits on the Santa Cruz River and may represent the Historic Pee Posh village of Hueso Parado (ca'kov'ªau' or Shakuvhál) or one of its satellite settlements (Russell 1908:22). Ceramics and historic artifacts collected from a recent survey of this site indicate that the area was occupied from around A.D. 1850 until the 1950s (Eiselt et al. 2002:467–479). While these two historic villages may have been established by different cultural groups in the eighteenth and nineteenth centuries, they both contain evidence for substantial prehistoric Hohokam occupation, especially during the late Classic.

It is important to note that, if GR-909 and GR-1139 represent the remains of settlement of two distinct ethnic groups (as suggested by the ethnohistoric literature), then artifact styles may be found to differ between these sites. For example, the projectile point collections from both sites contrast with regard to point style (Loendorf and Rice 2004; Randolph et al. 2002; see Figure 5). At GR-909, the proportion of Straight Base Triangular points (thought to be associated with Pima groups) is nearly three times higher than that from GR-1139, where U-shaped Base Triangular points (thought to be associated with Sobaipuri groups) dominate the assemblage. If these differences also are manifest in the pottery assemblages at these two sites, then GR-1139 may be expected to contain greater assemblage proportions of Sobaipuri Plain and Whetstone Plain wares. For example, pottery assemblages might mirror the distinction noted by Deaver (1990:15.17–15.18) between Ceramic Complex 1 (from Frog Pot) and Ceramic Complex 2 (from Whimsy Flat) in the western part of the middle Gila basin. While temporally distinct, pottery representing Complex 1 tends to resemble Sobaipuri types, including Whetstone Plain, while those of Complex 2 tend to resemble Patayan ceramics. Clearly, more detailed ceramic analysis of the plain ware assemblage is needed for GR-909 and GR-1139.

CHAPTER 4

QUANTITATIVE MEASURES FOR IDENTIFYING PROTOHISTORIC CERAMIC ASSEMBLAGES

The recent full-coverage pedestrian survey of the middle Gila River Valley by the Cultural Resource Management Program has gathered a large quantity of surface collection data, much of which consists of pottery. If we wish to understand better the period of transition between prehistory and history along the middle Gila, then it is necessary to develop techniques to analyze the different classes of survey data available, especially ceramics. For example, ceramic collections from surveyed sites can be compared against those from late Classic and early Historic sites to determine whether a given site or feature in the middle Gila region dates to the Protohistoric. In this way, sites likely to contain Protohistoric features can be identified for further investigation.

SAMPLING PROCEDURES

For this study, ceramic data from the middle Gila survey are compared with those from excavated sites in the Phoenix Basin (Table 4). I considered three sites containing Hopi yellow wares and O'odham projectile points (GR-355, GR-909, and GR-1139), along with three sites that do not contain yellow ware pottery (GR-493, GR-782, and GR-807); all six sites contain evidence for late Classic and early or late Historic occupation. There are several problems immediately apparent with this kind of study. First, assemblages from excavation and survey are differentially affected by geomorphologic and taphonomic processes in contrasting post-depositional environments, which may lead to differences in artifact preservation and movement (Lyman 1994; Schiffer 1972, 1987; Wood and Johnson 1978). However, it has been shown that lateral movement due to post-depositional disturbance is not as great in many circumstances as one might expect (Dunnell and Dancey 1983; Lewarch and O'Brien 1981; O'Brien and Lewarch 1982; Roper 1976; Trubowitz 1978). Second, differences in sampling design also can affect our understanding about the context of the artifact assemblages (Orton 2000:67–147). Finally, it is often the case that much more information is known about site structure and function from excavation compared with survey. Nevertheless, while different sampling methodologies limit the range of comparisons that can be made between excavation and survey data, it is a useful exercise because the results can, at the very least, indicate potential sites or features that merit further scrutiny.

Middle Gila Survey Data

The recent full-coverage archaeological survey conducted by the Gila River Indian Community's Cultural Resource Management Program presents an ideal opportunity to test ideas about Protohistoric ceramic assemblages. The survey, which included intensive surface collections at many of the more than 1,000 recorded sites, covers an area of roughly 525 km^2

Table 4. Sources of Ceramic Assemblage Data.

Site	Code	Location	Date Range	Reference
Casa Buena, Locus 1 (Stage 1), AZ T:12:37 (ASM)	CB	Phoenix Basin	1100-1450	Cable and Gould 1988:272
Pueblo Salado (Areas 15 and 16), AZ T:12:47 (ASM)	PS1	Phoenix Basin	1200-1400	Walsh-Anduze 1996a:87, 89
Pueblo Salado (Area 6), AZ T:12:47 (ASM)	PS2	Phoenix Basin	1200-1400	Walsh-Anduze 1996b:98, 106
Pueblo Patricio (all Classic features)	PP1	Phoenix Basin	1200-1450	Henderson 1995:80, 94
Pueblo Grande (all Civano features), AZ U:9:7 (ASM)	PG1	Phoenix Basin	1250-1350	Abbott 1994:10
Pueblo Grande (all Polvorón features), AZ U:9:7 (ASM)	PG2	Phoenix Basin	1350-1450	Abbott 1994:10
El Polvorón (ID only), AZ U:15:59 (ASM)	EP	Queen Creek drainage	1350-1450	Sires 1984:265-273
Frog Pot (Feature 15), AZ T:16:23 (ASM)	FP	Ak-Chin Indian Community	late 1600s-1890	Cable 1990:23.7
Painted Horse (Feature 1)	PH	Ak-Chin Indian Community	late 1600s-1890	Cable 1990:23.7
Site 55 (Feature 1)	55	Ak-Chin Indian Community	late 1600s-1890	Cable 1990:23.7
Site 86 (Homestead 4)	86	Ak-Chin Indian Community	late 1600s-1890	Cable 1990:23.7
Whimsy Flat (Structures 1-6), AZ T:16:71 (ASM)	WF	Ak-Chin Indian Community	late 1600s-1890	Cable 1990:23.7
Pueblo Patricio (all historic features)	PP2	Phoenix Basin	1880-1910	Henderson 1995:80-81
Alicia, AZ U:13:31 (ASU)	AL	Gila Crossing	1900-1914	Rice et al. 1983:79-80
AZ U:9:44 (ASM)	44	near I-10 and Maricopa Road	1903-1920	Ravesloot et al. 1992:67-69
GR-355	355	Casa Blanca, GRIC	various	Eiselt et al. 2002:702-703
GR-493	493	Casa Blanca, GRIC	various	Eiselt et al. 2002:726
GR-782	782	Casa Blanca, GRIC	various	Eiselt et al. 2002:753-755
GR-807	807	Casa Blanca, GRIC	various	Eiselt et al. 2002:758-760
GR-909	909	Casa Blanca, GRIC	various	GRIC artifact database
GR-1139	1139	Casa Blanca, GRIC	various	Eiselt et al. 2002:768-773
GR-1139, Locus A	A	Casa Blanca, GRIC	unknown	Eiselt et al. 2002:768
GR-1139, Locus B	B	Casa Blanca, GRIC	unknown	Eiselt et al. 2002:768
GR-1139, Locus C	C	Casa Blanca, GRIC	unknown	Eiselt et al. 2002:768-769
GR-1139, Locus D	D	Casa Blanca, GRIC	unknown	Eiselt et al. 2002:769
GR-1139, Locus E	E	Casa Blanca, GRIC	unknown	Eiselt et al. 2002:769
GR-1139, Locus F	F	Casa Blanca, GRIC	unknown	Eiselt et al. 2002:769
GR-1139, Locus G	G	Casa Blanca, GRIC	unknown	Eiselt et al. 2002:769-770
GR-1139, Locus H	H	Casa Blanca, GRIC	unknown	Eiselt et al. 2002:770
GR-1139, Locus I	I	Casa Blanca, GRIC	unknown	Eiselt et al. 2002:770
GR-1139, Locus J	J	Casa Blanca, GRIC	unknown	Eiselt et al. 2002:770
GR-1139, Locus K	K	Casa Blanca, GRIC	unknown	Eiselt et al. 2002:771
GR-1139, Locus L	L	Casa Blanca, GRIC	unknown	Eiselt et al. 2002:771
GR-1139, Locus M	M	Casa Blanca, GRIC	unknown	Eiselt et al. 2002:771
GR-1139, Locus N	N	Casa Blanca, GRIC	unknown	Eiselt et al. 2002:771-772
GR-1139, Locus O	O	Casa Blanca, GRIC	unknown	Eiselt et al. 2002:772
GR-1139, Locus P	P	Casa Blanca, GRIC	unknown	Eiselt et al. 2002:772
GR-1139, Locus Q	Q	Casa Blanca, GRIC	unknown	Eiselt et al. 2002:772-773
GR-1139, Locus R	R	Casa Blanca, GRIC	unknown	Eiselt et al. 2002:773
GR-1139, Locus S	S	Casa Blanca, GRIC	unknown	Eiselt et al. 2002:773

(approximately 130,000 acres). We utilize three surface-collection strategies during site recording: general, quantitative, and diagnostic (see Orton 2000; Redman 1978, 1987; Redman and Watson 1970). Selection of a specific strategy is based on the number and distribution of artifacts, as well as the presence of temporally diagnostic artifacts such as identifiable prehistoric decorated ceramic types or historic artifacts with a maker's mark (Doyel and Green 1995).

For sites with fewer than 100 artifacts, such as small artifact scatters with a low probability of containing subsurface cultural deposits or features, diagnostic artifacts are point-provenienced and all remaining visible artifacts are collected as a "general" collection. "Quantitative" collections are judgmental samples taken at sites with 100 or more artifacts. Each quantitative collection unit consists of a circle with a 2-m diameter, created using two nails attached to a 1-m length of string. At sites with widely dispersed artifact scatters, a maximum of three quantitative collection units per site—or per locus if two or more loci are present—are situated in order to obtain the requisite 100 artifacts in a timely manner. At larger sites with multiple cultural features and deposits, such as villages, additional quantitative collection units are judgmentally placed within each of these areas to further define the functional and temporal character of the site. "Diagnostic" collections, made after quantitative collections are completed, consist of judgmental collections from identified features and loci. Diagnostic collections provide additional sources of information to supplement temporally sensitive artifacts sampled from quantitative collection units. All ceramics are analyzed by assigning each sherd to a particular ware designation (plain, red, brown, buff, or polychrome) based on surface finish and paste type. These ware categories were assigned for general classificatory purposes, and allow comparison with other data.

Comparative Ceramic Data

Comparative ceramic data derive from 14 excavated sites in the Phoenix Basin: four Classic period (about A.D. 1100 to 1400) sites, two inferred Polvorón phase (about A.D. 1350 to 1450) settlements, five early Historic (about A.D. late 1600s to 1880) occupations, and three late Historic (about A.D. 1880 to 1920) homesteads. Table 5 presents the raw data used in this study. As shown in the table, sample size varies greatly among data sets, from 99 to roughly 60,000 sherds per site. However, sample size variance is much lower among sites of the same time period (Table 6). The variables (ceramic wares) selected for study include those consistently reported by ceramic analysts: Plain (all plain wares), Red (all red wares), Brown (including Red-on-brown types), Buff (including Red-on-buff types), Polychrome (usually Salado polychromes for Classic period sites), and Other (a variable category, mainly composed of rare and intrusive types).

Classic period assemblages derive from the sites of Casa Buena, Pueblo Salado (two separate loci), Pueblo Patricio, and Pueblo Grande. Each of these sites represents a large platform mound community with adobe-walled compounds in the central Phoenix Basin. Most data come from Civano phase occupations (about A.D. 1300 to 1450), although the assemblage from Casa Buena has Soho phase (about A.D. 1150 to 1300) materials mixed into

Table 5. Sample Matrix for Ceramic Assemblage Data.

Site[a]	Plain n	Plain %[b]	Red n	Red %	Brown n	Brown %	Buff n	Buff %	Polychrome n	Polychrome %	Other n	Other %	Total
CB	9043	65	4697	34	0	0	145	1	51	0	0	0	13936
PS1	645	69	217	23	0	0	65	7	2	0	0	0	929
PS2	8437	81	1703	16	1	0	120	1	149	1	16	0	10426
PP1	2319	92	150	6	0	0	24	1	39	2	0	0	2532
PG1	46869	79	10172	17	0	0	608	1	474	1	1239	2	59362
PG2	25498	71	8288	23	0	0	560	2	889	2	538	2	35773
EP	28822	52	22077	40	319	1	181	0	4323	8	57	0	55779
FP	150	95	0	0	0	0	4	3	0	0	4	3	158
PH	184	81	0	0	0	0	21	9	0	0	21	9	226
55	105	100	0	0	0	0	0	0	0	0	0	0	105
86	126	100	0	0	0	0	0	0	0	0	0	0	126
WF	140	100	0	0	0	0	0	0	0	0	0	0	140
PP2	383	84	40	9	0	0	23	5	9	2	0	0	455
AL	678	38	353	20	231	13	530	30	0	0	0	0	1792
44	99	100	0	0	0	0	0	0	0	0	0	0	99
355	183	46	34	9	10	3	166	42	6	2	0	0	399
493	198	40	41	8	1	0	238	49	11	2	0	0	489
782	1991	36	685	12	257	5	2637	47	25	0	0	0	5595
807	510	45	216	19	8	1	372	33	19	2	0	0	1125
909	8462	28	6330	21	4192	14	10766	36	5	0	0	0	29755
1139	2066	59	912	26	18	1	473	13	44	1	0	0	3513
Total	136908	61	55915	25	5037	2	16933	8	6046	3	1875	1	222714
A	37	100	0	0	0	0	0	0	0	0	0	0	37
B	42	67	0	0	0	0	21	33	0	0	0	0	63
C	111	69	15	9	0	0	33	21	1	1	0	0	160
D	243	68	47	13	7	2	23	6	38	11	0	0	358
E	3	100	0	0	0	0	0	0	0	0	0	0	3
F	26	100	0	0	0	0	0	0	0	0	0	0	26
G	21	100	0	0	0	0	0	0	0	0	0	0	21
H	15	88	0	0	0	0	2	12	0	0	0	0	17
I	64	100	0	0	0	0	0	0	0	0	0	0	64
J	11	100	0	0	0	0	0	0	0	0	0	0	11
K	114	77	8	5	0	0	26	18	0	0	0	0	148
L	450	48	376	40	11	1	97	10	0	0	0	0	934
M	0	0	3	100	0	0	0	0	0	0	0	0	3
N	86	50	8	5	0	0	78	45	0	0	0	0	172
O	34	68	11	22	0	0	5	10	0	0	0	0	50
P	130	31	265	63	0	0	25	6	0	0	0	0	420
Q	7	47	2	13	0	0	6	40	0	0	0	0	15
R	29	63	0	0	0	0	17	37	0	0	0	0	46
S	1	9	0	0	0	0	10	91	0	0	0	0	11
Total	1424	56	735	29	18	1	343	13	39	2	0	0	2559

[a]refer to Table 4 for code designations

[b]row percents

Table 6. Summary Statistics for Ceramic Assemblage Data.

Site	n	μ	σ	cv[a]
Classic	87185.0	17437.0	24050.9	137.9
Polvorón	91552.0	45776.0	14146.4	30.9
early Historic	755.0	151.0	46.2	30.6
late Historic	2346.0	782.0	892.6	114.1
GRIC	40876.0	6812.7	11421.0	167.6

[a]cv=coefficient of variation, calculated by the standard deviation (σ) divided by the mean (μ) multiplied by 100

some Civano features. Data from Polvorón phase collections were taken from reports on El Polvorón and Pueblo Grande. Significantly, El Polvorón is a small, single-phase farmstead, while Pueblo Grande is an exceptionally large platform mound community, although it is uncertain to what extent Classic period buildings were occupied during the Polvorón phase at this site. Early Historic materials are represented by excavation in the Ak-Chin Indian Community, located in the southwest Phoenix Basin: Frog Pot, Painted Horse, Site 55, Site 86, and Whimsy Flat. With the exception of Whimsy Flat, all of these sites are small, *ranchería*-style settlements. Whimsy Flat is a possible village with as many as 40 structures, although not all appear to have been occupied contemporaneously. Finally, late Historic pottery data were collected from the sites of Alicia, Pueblo Patricio, and AZ U:9:44 (ASM), each of which is a small homestead with a limited occupation of only a few decades.

ANALYTICAL METHODS

In this section, multivariate quantitative assessments of ceramic assemblage data produced from excavations of late Classic and Historic sites in the Phoenix Basin are evaluated against data from multiple-component sites investigated as part of the middle Gila survey to determine if possible Protohistoric materials can be detected among Classic and Historic deposits. First, I employ Correspondence Analysis to determine if any of the ceramic collections in the study are similar to one another and to explore the ways in which similar collections might be related. Next, I examine Brainerd-Robinson similarity coefficients to assess the degree to which certain assemblages are similar to one another. In this way, it may be possible to establish which sites in the middle Gila survey have the greatest potential to contain Protohistoric remains for more detailed investigation.

Correspondence Analysis

For comparing ceramic assemblages, I employ Correspondence Analysis (CA) to examine the ways in which collections are related (see Bertelsen 1988; Bølviken 1982; Clouse 1999; Greenacre 1994). This multivariate analytical technique is designed to analyze occurrence frequency data in a two-way contingency table to show a graphical representation of the two-dimensional relationships (viewed on a scatter plot) between cases, between variables, and between cases and variables. The analysis produces a graphical display of the rows and columns of the data matrix, illustrating clusters within the rows and within the columns, as well as the association between them; here, both cases and variables are plotted together. Importantly, the analysis reduces domination by frequency counts and focuses on relationships between groups of objects and their context. This capability helps to overcome the fact that in situations where some variables have significantly higher frequencies than others, the variation in the former will tend to dominate the analysis and the variation in the latter will have very little effect on it. In addition, the multivariate nature of CA can reveal relationships that would not be detected in a series of pairwise comparisons of a variable, such as with Pearson's linear correlation coefficients or Brainerd-Robinson similarity coefficients.

If two sets of cases (ceramic assemblages) are similar in the composition of ceramic wares, then they will appear close to one another on the scatter plot. Likewise, if a case and a variable (ceramic wares) are similar, then these will tend to appear close to one another on the plot as well. In this way, the relationships (based on the frequencies of ceramic wares in a given assemblage) among assemblages can be compared to one another, as well as their relationships to ceramic wares. Thus, this analysis can determine the relative strength of a relationship between assemblages along with the ways in which the assemblages are similar.

Figure 8 shows a scatter plot of the first and second component scores for a CA I performed on the ceramic ware frequency data (n = 222,714). The first three components account for 97.8 percent of the variance. The variables are labeled with solid squares, while the cases are represented by different geometric symbols. The plot shows three spatially discrete clusters and two outliers. One cluster consists of most of the Gila River sites, save for GR-1139, a complex multiple-component site. This group plots close to the buff ware variable, suggesting that the proportion of buff wares is different among these assemblages relative to other assemblages in the study. The second group is composed mostly of late Classic sites, along with the Polvorón phase occupation at Pueblo Grande. These cases cluster around the plain ware variable, suggesting that plain ware proportions are important in distinguishing this group from others.

The third cluster is composed mainly of early Historic sites, in addition to the late Historic assemblage from AZ U:9:44 (ASM). These assemblages appear to be distinguished from others in the study by the proportion of "other" ceramic wares, suggesting that the early Historic sites are less variable in ceramic diversity compared with the Classic sites in the study. However, four of these assemblages (from Site 55, Site 86, Whimsy Flat, and AZ U:9:44 [ASM]) are composed entirely of plain ware pottery. Finally, both Alicia and El Polvorón are not associated with any group. Notably, El Polvorón appears to be distinguished from the other assemblages in the study by the proportion of red wares in its assemblage, an observation originally noted by Sires (1984:269). It is important to point out that similarities among some of the assemblages may be a factor of geography. For example, all of the late Classic sites are located in the central Phoenix Basin, and all of the early Historic sites are in the Ak-Chin Indian Community in the southwestern part of the basin.

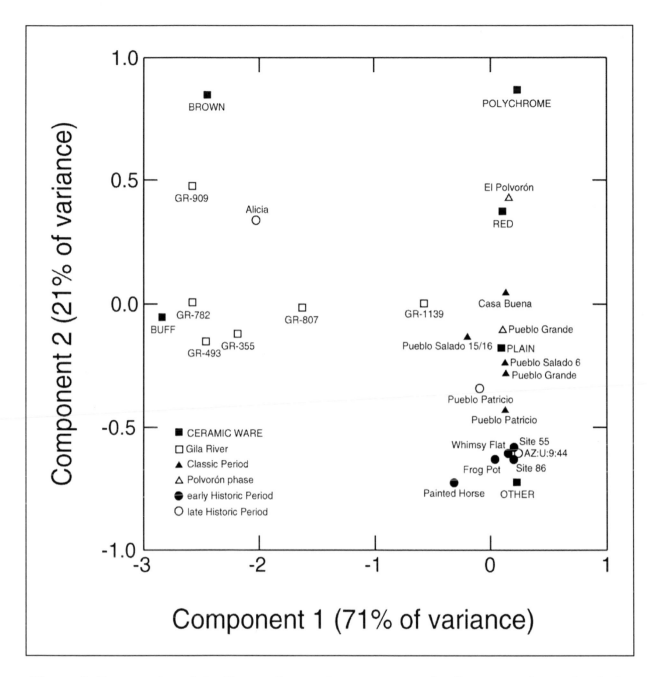

Figure 8. Scatter plot of the first and second components of a Correspondence Analysis comparing the ceramic assemblages from GRIC survey sites to sites representing various periods in southern Arizona ($\chi^2 = 79826.9$, $df = 95$, $p = 0.000$).

As noted above, the CA plot classifies Site GR-1139, a multiple-component (prehistoric and historic) occupation, as a Classic period site. This is likely the case because of the scale and complexity of GR-1139 relative to the other Gila River sites in the study. A total of 19 different activity loci were recorded at GR-1139, some of which appear to be temporally distinct (Eiselt et al. 2002:469). At GR-1139, five loci (K, L, M, N, and P) encompass the habitation component of a late Historic (about A.D. 1850 to 1950) village.

Five smaller loci (E, F, G, H, and I) are each composed of temporally indeterminate artifact scatters characterized by a relative abundance of lithics and plain ware ceramics. Archaic period (about 2550 to 2050 B.C.) deposits appear in four loci (D, O, P, and R). Six loci (A, B, C, J, O, and Q) contain temporally mixed artifact distributions that include Archaic, Hohokam, and O'odham materials. Finally, temporally indeterminate bedrock mortars and cupules and a series of depressions extend across several small hills in three loci (Q, R, and S). Given the complexity of GR-1139, it is useful to consider its component loci separately in another CA.

Figure 9 shows a scatter plot of the first and second component scores for a CA I conducted on the ceramic ware frequency data from each locus at GR-1139, along with the comparative assemblages from the Phoenix Basin sites (n = 184,397). The first three components account for 95.7 percent of the variance. The plot shows three clusters and one outlier (Locus P). The first group (Loci B, N, Q, and R) does not appear to correspond to any site in the study. This may be explained by the composition of the ceramic assemblages from these loci, which contain only plain and buff ware ceramics. The second group (Loci A, E, G, I, J, and possibly C, H, and K) plots near the early Historic sites. These loci have assemblages composed mostly of plain wares, although Locus A contains roughly 30 percent buff wares. The third group (Loci D, L, and O) plots close to Classic period sites, although the assemblages associated with these loci have markedly different proportions of ceramic wares. While their association with the Classic sites is unclear, the relationship could be a product of assemblage diversity. The three loci and the Classic sites have very diverse assemblages relative to other loci from GR-1139.

Brainerd-Robinson Similarity Coefficient Analysis

The discreteness of the spatial patterns generated by the CA suggests that some Gila River sites and some loci within GR-1139 may contain Protohistoric materials. It is therefore useful to examine the extent to which the collections from these and other sites are similar to one another, that is, to determine the relative strength of the similarities. For comparing ceramic assemblages, I calculated Brainerd-Robinson Similarity Coefficients (*br*) to assess the degree to which collections are similar (Brainerd 1951; Robinson 1951). Originally devised for measuring similarity between pottery assemblages described in percentages of different types, the statistic totals the absolute value of the differences of the type percentages between defined categories for pairs of assemblages (Brainerd 1951; Cowgill 1990; Doran and Hodson 1975; Robinson 1951). By subtracting any calculated difference from 200, an equivalent measure of similarity is obtained. The formula is:

$$br_{AB} = 200 - \Sigma \ (i = 1 \text{ to } N) \left| P_{iA} - P_{iB} \right|$$

where P_{iA} is the percentage representation of attribute or type i in assemblage A, and P_{iB} is the percentage representation of attribute or type i in assemblage B. The sum of the differences is subtracted from 200, because the maximum possible "distance" between two

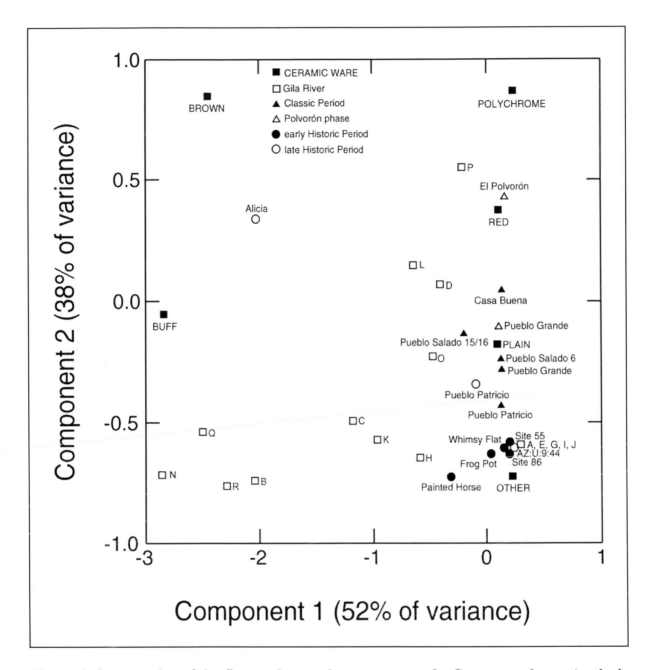

Figure 9. Scatter plot of the first and second components of a Correspondence Analysis comparing the ceramic assemblage from excavation loci at Site GR-1139 to those of sites representing various periods in southern Arizona (χ^2 = 45025.4, df = 165, p = 0.000).

collections, based on percentages, is 200. Thus, a *br* value of 200 represents the highest possible similarity, while zero represents the lowest possible similarity. For more intuitive results, I scaled the *br* coefficient by dividing the statistic by 200; thus, a *br* value of 1 represents identical assemblages while a *br* value of zero represents totally different assemblages.

One potential problem with this statistic is that, since it is based on comparing percentages, a particular *br* coefficient value could be based on the two assemblages having fairly similar percents of all categories, or extremely similar percents for most categories and quite different percents for a few categories (Cowgill 1990). As a result, it is necessary to examine the raw data sets in all cases and to specify the conditions upon which the degree of similarity is based. The *br* statistic is used in this study because ceramic information is reported in the survey data as counts of types, which easily convert into percentages of types with respect to entire collections. In addition, Cowgill (1990) has pointed out some of the problems with using other kinds of correlation procedures for this purpose, such as Pearson's coefficient of linear correlation. He suggests that other statistics, such as the *br* coefficient, are preferable when comparing collections characterized by their percents of different ceramic types.

Table 7 presents a *br* coefficient matrix comparing all samples in the study. The matrix shows that there are strong similarities (i.e., *br* ≥ .80) among the assemblages from Classic period sites (Casa Buena, Pueblo Salado, Pueblo Patricio, and Pueblo Grande), which are also quite similar to the Polvorón phase assemblage from Pueblo Grande. The greatest differences among assemblages in this group are in the proportions of buff wares, brown wares, and polychromes. Notably, the assemblage from the site of El Polvorón is not as similar to these collections as the Pueblo Grande Polvorón materials. This could be the case because El Polvorón is a small farmstead site, functionally different from Pueblo Grande, a large platform mound community (see Hackbarth 1995:178–179). Pueblo Grande also contains multiple phase components, such that separating out individual Polvorón phase assemblages is difficult (see Abbott 1994).

The matrix also shows similarities in ceramic assemblages among the early Historic sites from the Ak-Chin Indian Community (Frog Pot, Painted Horse, Site 55, Site 86, and Whimsy Flat), which are all different (i.e., *br* ≤ .50) from the Classic period assemblages. In this group, the greatest assemblage differences are expressed in the frequencies of buff wares, brown wares, and polychromes—an expected pattern since most of these assemblages are composed entirely of plain ware ceramics. While the assemblage from the late Historic site of AZ U:9:44 (ASM) is highly similar to those from the early Historic sites (μ *br* = .95), the ceramic collection from the late Historic site of Alicia is markedly different from these sites (μ *br* = .40). Indeed, the assemblage from Alicia, which includes higher proportions of buff wares and brown wares relative to the other assemblages, is different from all other samples in the study. Generally, the results suggest that Protohistoric sites may be distinguishable from Classic sites based on the proportions of ceramic wares. Ceramic collections from sites representing the El Polvorón phase, however, are indistinguishable from those from Classic sites based on their *br* coefficients.

The sites from the Gila River Indian Community are all highly similar (*br* ≥ .73), save for GR-1139, which is more similar to the Classic period assemblages (μ *br* = .79), a finding that parallels the results of the CA. Thus, it is useful to consider GR-1139 loci separately for this analysis. Table 8 presents a *br* matrix comparing the ceramic assemblages from the 19 loci at GR-1139 against the comparative assemblages. The assemblages from Loci E through K and possibly Q, which include 80 to 100 percent plain wares, have strong

Table 7. Brainerd-Robinson Similarity Coefficient Matrix Comparing Ceramic Assemblages among Archaeological Sites in South-central Arizona.

	CB	PS1	PS2	PP1	PG1	PG2	EP	FP	PH	55	86	WF	PP2	AL	44	355	493	782	807	909	1139
CB	1.00																				
PS1	0.90	1.00																			
PS2	0.83	0.87	1.00																		
PP1	0.72	0.77	0.89	1.00																	
PG1	0.83	0.87	0.98	0.87	1.00																
PG2	0.89	0.94	0.90	0.80	0.91	1.00															
EP	0.86	0.76	0.70	0.59	0.69	0.78	1.00														
FP	0.66	0.72	0.82	0.93	0.83	0.74	0.52	1.00													
PH	0.66	0.76	0.82	0.82	0.83	0.74	0.52	0.86	1.00												
55	0.65	0.69	0.81	0.92	0.79	0.71	0.52	0.95	0.81	1.00											
86	0.65	0.69	0.81	0.92	0.79	0.71	0.52	0.95	0.81	1.00	1.00										
WF	0.65	0.69	0.81	0.92	0.79	0.71	0.52	0.95	0.81	1.00	1.00	1.00									
PP2	0.75	0.83	0.92	0.93	0.90	0.84	0.63	0.87	0.86	0.84	0.84	0.84	1.00								
AL	0.59	0.65	0.55	0.45	0.55	0.59	0.58	0.40	0.47	0.38	0.38	0.38	0.52	1.00							
44	0.65	0.69	0.81	0.92	0.79	0.71	0.52	0.95	0.81	1.00	1.00	1.00	0.84	0.38	1.00						
355	0.56	0.62	0.57	0.54	0.55	0.57	0.57	0.48	0.55	0.46	0.46	0.46	0.61	0.78	0.46	1.00					
493	0.50	0.56	0.51	0.49	0.50	0.53	0.52	0.43	0.50	0.40	0.40	0.40	0.56	0.76	0.40	0.92	1.00				
782	0.49	0.55	0.49	0.43	0.48	0.50	0.49	0.38	0.45	0.36	0.36	0.36	0.50	0.82	0.36	0.89	0.92	1.00			
807	0.66	0.72	0.64	0.54	0.64	0.68	0.67	0.48	0.55	0.45	0.45	0.45	0.61	0.87	0.45	0.89	0.84	0.82	1.00		
909	0.51	0.57	0.46	0.35	0.46	0.51	0.51	0.31	0.38	0.28	0.28	0.28	0.42	0.91	0.28	0.76	0.73	0.81	0.81	1.00	
1139	0.86	0.89	0.78	0.67	0.77	0.85	0.80	0.61	0.68	0.59	0.59	0.59	0.74	0.72	0.59	0.70	0.64	0.62	0.80	0.64	1.00

Note : refer to Table 4 for code designations.

similarities with those from the early and late Historic sites (br = .81–1.00), along with the Classic occupation at Pueblo Patricio (br = .83–.92). The ceramic collections from Loci D and O have their strongest similarities to the collections from Classic period sites (br = .84–.97, where the greatest differences are in the proportions of red wares). The ceramics from El Polvorón, which include plain and red wares in roughly equal proportions, are similarly distributed as those from Loci L and M (br = .87–.88). Finally, the remaining loci (A through C, N, and P through S) do not have strong similarity coefficients with any of the sites in the study. Overall, the results suggest that there is some degree of internal patterning among the loci at GR-1139 with respect to the distribution of ceramic wares, which may have temporal correlations.

Table 8. Brainerd-Robinson Similarity Coefficient Matrix Comparing Ceramic Assemblages from Site GR-1139 with Those from Sites in South-central Arizona.

	CB	PS1	PS2	PP1	PG1	PG2	EP	FP	PH	55	86	WF	PP2	AL	44
A	0.67	0.77	0.72	0.72	0.71	0.73	0.53	0.73	0.79	0.70	0.70	0.70	0.76	0.68	0.70
B	0.66	0.74	0.68	0.68	0.67	0.69	0.52	0.70	0.76	0.67	0.67	0.67	0.72	0.67	0.67
C	0.75	0.85	0.80	0.77	0.79	0.81	0.62	0.72	0.78	0.69	0.69	0.69	0.84	0.68	0.69
D	0.79	0.87	0.84	0.76	0.82	0.85	0.73	0.71	0.74	0.68	0.68	0.68	0.84	0.59	0.68
E	0.65	0.69	0.81	0.92	0.79	0.71	0.52	0.95	0.81	1.00	1.00	1.00	0.84	0.38	1.00
F	0.65	0.69	0.81	0.92	0.79	0.71	0.52	0.95	0.81	1.00	1.00	1.00	0.84	0.38	1.00
G	0.65	0.69	0.81	0.92	0.79	0.71	0.52	0.95	0.81	1.00	1.00	1.00	0.84	0.38	1.00
H	0.66	0.76	0.82	0.89	0.80	0.73	0.52	0.91	0.91	0.88	0.88	0.88	0.89	0.50	0.88
I	0.65	0.69	0.81	0.92	0.79	0.71	0.52	0.95	0.81	1.00	1.00	1.00	0.84	0.38	1.00
J	0.67	0.78	0.84	0.91	0.82	0.75	0.54	0.91	0.91	0.88	0.88	0.88	0.91	0.49	0.88
K	0.71	0.81	0.83	0.83	0.82	0.78	0.57	0.80	0.86	0.77	0.77	0.77	0.87	0.61	0.77
L	0.83	0.78	0.65	0.55	0.66	0.73	0.88	0.51	0.57	0.48	0.48	0.48	0.62	0.70	0.48
M	0.82	0.71	0.64	0.54	0.65	0.71	0.87	0.48	0.48	0.47	0.47	0.47	0.57	0.59	0.47
N	0.56	0.62	0.56	0.56	0.55	0.57	0.55	0.53	0.59	0.50	0.50	0.50	0.60	0.72	0.50
O	0.88	0.97	0.85	0.75	0.86	0.92	0.74	0.71	0.77	0.68	0.68	0.68	0.82	0.68	0.68
P	0.66	0.60	0.48	0.38	0.49	0.56	0.71	0.34	0.37	0.31	0.31	0.31	0.45	0.57	0.31
Q	0.70	0.76	0.70	0.60	0.69	0.71	0.68	0.56	0.62	0.53	0.53	0.53	0.67	0.83	0.53
R	0.64	0.70	0.64	0.64	0.63	0.65	0.52	0.66	0.72	0.63	0.63	0.63	0.68	0.67	0.63
S	0.54	0.60	0.54	0.51	0.53	0.55	0.53	0.47	0.53	0.44	0.44	0.44	0.58	0.76	0.44

Note: refer to Table 4 for code designations.

CHAPTER 5

POTENTIAL CONTRIBUTIONS OF PROTOHISTORIC STUDIES

The archaeology of the Protohistoric period remains poorly understood throughout south-central Arizona, despite recent efforts to improve chronological resolution and to re-evaluate some of the diagnostic criteria used to identify Protohistoric remains in the archaeological record. As a result, the primary source of information for the Protohistoric is Spanish documentary materials, which describe the distribution and lifestyles of Sonoran Desert cultures of the early Historic period. More archaeological data from this period as well as from the Protohistoric are needed from across southern and central Arizona to understand better the historical trajectory of the pre-Hispanic Hohokam and historic Pima groups. The quantitative analyses introduced in this study provide one means to identify sites that may yield Protohistoric materials upon further investigation.

RESEARCH QUESTIONS

Research issues that can be addressed with better chronological resolution and improved site or feature identification include: processes of abandonment of Civano phase villages, development of the *ranchería*-style residential pattern, geographic distribution of Protohistoric settlement, realignments of regional and interregional social networks during the early Protohistoric period, changes in material culture and technology that accompanied the reorganization of Hohokam groups, restructuring of Classic period social and political organization, shifts in irrigation and *ak-chin* subsistence practices, and historical continuity with modern groups in southern and central Arizona, among others. Due to the highly fragmented and incomplete nature of data available to address any of these topics, most research questions are framed best in terms of regional phenomena. That is, no single site has relevant information on all or even most aspects needed to understand these issues and to develop a coherent set of testable implications for archaeological research. Some of the crucial research questions that have emerged from extant studies of the periods surrounding the Protohistoric include the following:

How did Protohistoric inhabitants of central Arizona respond to fluctuations in local ecological conditions during the fifteenth and sixteenth centuries? It has been suggested that the Civano phase represents a period of prolonged drought followed by a series of high-magnitude floods, which seriously impacted subsistence practices (Graybill et al. 1999; Graybill and Nials 1989; Huckleberry 1999; Nials et al. 1989; compare Waters and Ravesloot 2001). What social and technological changes resulted from these environmental shifts? How did post-Classic subsistence practices differ from Classic ones? If less agriculture was practiced during the post-Classic, did an increased reliance on hunting and gathering put pressure on certain faunal and floral taxa or on certain catchment areas? What is the relationship between post-Classic subsistence strategies and settlement patterns? These are significant questions because the answers bear directly on broader issues surrounding the reorganization of the Hohokam at the end of the Classic period.

How did Protohistoric groups respond to changes in regional economies during this time? It has been suggested that regional patterns of interaction, which had significant economic impacts on local communities, shifted during the end of the Classic period. Based on ceramic inventories from excavated sites, there are increased proportions of Salado polychromes (from the Tonto Basin and possibly from the Colorado Plateau and White Mountains regions) observed in the Phoenix Basin until around A.D. 1400 to 1450 (Abbott 2000; Crown 1994; Danson and Wallace 1956; Dittert and Plog 1980; Simon et al. 1998). After this time, the appearance of proto-Hopi yellow wares from northern Arizona and later, Zuni polychromes along with Little Colorado buff ware from northeastern Arizona/northwestern New Mexico, signals shifts in interregional ties (Crown 1983, 1984). In the Tucson Basin, however, after the Classic period, pottery resembles Mogollon styles and technologies seen in northern Sonora (Fish et al. 1992; Masse 1981; Pailes 1972, 1978). The nature of change in southern Arizona pottery assemblages needs to be understood better for the Protohistoric. This is a critical avenue of research that has important implications not only for explaining changes to Hohokam cultural traditions in the fifteenth century, but also for examining the question of Hohokam-Pima continuity.

In what ways and to what extent did Protohistoric populations articulate with groups in northern and western Mexico? Archaeologists working in the American Southwest have documented waves of Mesoamerican influence (see Mathien and McGuire 1986; Riley 1980), primarily during the late Pioneer period (about A.D. 600 to 800), as exhibited at Snaketown (Gladwin et al. 1937; Wilcox et al. 1981), and toward the end of the Classic period (about A.D. 1250 to 1450), as documented in Medio period assemblages at Paquimé (Di Peso 1974; Schaafsma and Riley 1999). What kinds of relationships existed between post-Classic populations in southern Arizona and those farther south in Mexico? Did these relationships affect the cultural trajectories of Protohistoric groups? These are important issues that require resolution if we are to understand long-term processes of culture change in southern Arizona.

How was Protohistoric settlement organized on a regional scale? Unlike previous and subsequent eras, there are few large settlements (i.e., concentrations of people greater than 500) evident in south-central Arizona during the Protohistoric period (compare Bolton 1948). Given this pattern of occupation, archaeologists have argued that the region was largely unoccupied. As Nelson (1999:11–12) points out, however, "regions may never have been completely abandoned in the past, but until considerable research is directed toward understanding the occupational histories of small settlements and the organization of land use that produced them, the nature and context of dispersed land use and its relationship to aggregated settlement in the Southwest will remain poorly understood." Small settlements, such as Protohistoric *rancherías* and early historic homesteads, need not imply short occupation spans (see Fish and Fish 1994; Kent 1992). One important question confronting Protohistoric research in Arizona is how dispersed settlement was organized on a regional scale. Were small hamlets occupied for long periods or were they seasonally occupied across different geomorphological or ecological environments? Also, how were these settlements connected physically across the landscape (e.g., Becker and Altschul 2003)?

What strategies characterized Protohistoric production economies? Since very little Protohistoric material culture has been unearthed, it is difficult to model production economies at individual sites in southern Arizona for this period. Some archaeologists have observed that, after the Classic period, obsidian became one of the most widely used lithic materials for tool manufacture (e.g., Chenault 1993; Howell 1993; Landis 1990; Sires 1984). Others have noted a decline in the importation of marine shell (e.g., Sires 1984; Vokes 1984). These patterns appear to vary from region to region, however. In addition to plain and red-slipped pottery and triangular projectile points, what material culture characterizes the Protohistoric? Which materials were consumed or traded and in what quantities? How and why did production technologies change over the course of the Protohistoric? Questions such as these need to be addressed in order to understand Protohistoric production economies. In addition, more information on the manufacture and technology of Protohistoric material culture may reveal additional diagnostic criteria useful for inferring and possibly dating Protohistoric occupations in the archaeological record (e.g., Loendorf and Rice 2004).

How did Protohistoric lifeways condition later interactions with Europeans? It has been suggested that the dispersed, *ranchería*-style settlement pattern of early historic groups in southern Arizona frustrated Spanish missionization efforts (Riley 1987:117–119). However, others argue that the low population densities, possibly a result of depopulation by disease (Dobyns 1963; Ezell 1961), enabled Spanish missionaries to acculturate Piman-speaking groups more quickly and with less resistance (Wilson 1999). These are untested propositions, however, that merit further scrutiny (see Majewski and Ayres 1997). While little is known about Protohistoric settlement patterns in the Phoenix Basin (Cable 1990:23.14–23.25), Spanish documents mention large villages in the Santa Cruz and San Pedro river valleys (Bolton 1948). It is therefore unclear how settlement size and distribution affected Spanish-indigenous interactions (see Ezell 1957). In what ways did the dispersed settlement pattern condition Spanish attempts to colonize groups in southern Arizona? In what ways did settlement systems work to preserve indigenous lifeways? How did settlement patterns affect the introduction of European crops and the transition to a mixed pastoral economy, and what recursive impacts did these changes have on settlement and land use? Clearly, more information is needed on these issues, at the very least because their resolution can assist with documenting diachronic shifts in settlement location and land-use practices in the region.

FUTURE DIRECTIONS

Given the complexity of micro-population movements and cultural interaction during and after the Classic period (Clark 2001; Duff 2002; Haury 1958; Lyons 2003; Teague 1989; Whittlesey 1997b), it is unlikely that any single population remained intact as a genetic and cultural unit (Teague 1989:152). Instead, variability characterizes Protohistoric settlement types and material assemblages. Ravesloot and Whittlesey (1987), for example, have found that post-Classic projectile point types are highly standardized within sites in the Tucson Basin but exhibit a great deal of variance when compared to other sites. Similarly, in the southwestern Phoenix Basin, Deaver (1990) notes that early Historic pottery styles and assemblage compositions are highly similar among sites in the Ak-Chin farms area but are significantly different from comparable collections elsewhere in the basin. Ultimately, identifying Protohistoric remains relies on recognizing a constellation of material culture patterns; there are no Protohistoric hallmark traits. As the current study suggests, this can be accomplished with multivariate assessments of the data, including exploratory data analysis.

Collection of additional archaeological data from Protohistoric contexts can address many of the research questions posed above. To do this, however, a concerted effort needs to be made to identify those contexts and to understand their temporal place within broader Hohokam and Pima chronologies. The quantitative exercises presented in this report evaluate the degree to which ceramic assemblages from documented late Classic and early Historic sites are similar to those from sites and deposits of unknown or uncertain date along the middle Gila. In this way, the technique sets up a method for detecting sites, as well as deposits in multiple-component sites, that may date to the Protohistoric period. The technique is less successful, however, at discerning Polvorón phase occupations.

The quantitative studies presented in this report identify plain, buff, and red ware proportions in ceramic assemblages as potentially useful indicators for detecting Protohistoric sites. As such, it may be possible to identify middle Gila sites that are likely candidates for containing Protohistoric remains based on simple trivariate plots of ceramic frequency data with these variables as axes (Figure 10). In this plot, possible Protohistoric sites contain from 30 to 50 percent buff ware and the rest plain ware. These assemblages contrast with those from Classic period sites, which have almost no buff ware, but trade off plain and red ware from about 55-45 to about 90-10 percent. Early historic sites have no red ware, but are overwhelmingly composed of plain ware with no more than 10 percent buff ware.

If this kind of plot accurately reflects temporal associations among sites, then Figure 10 reveals that Sites GR-355, GR-493, GR-782, GR-807, and GR-909 (and possibly Alicia) have potential to contain Protohistoric components. This kind of plot is not successful, however, at identifying Protohistoric deposits at more complex sites, such as GR-1139, where individual loci need to be evaluated separately. In addition, the technique may not work with small sample sizes (see Chase 1985; Cowgill 1964; Rhode 1988). Nevertheless, given the analytical potential of these kinds of studies, similar investigations need to be conducted on the relationships of paste type frequencies among Protohistoric sites, since it has been suggested that the proportions of certain plain ware temper types, such as phyllite, schist, and sand, are temporally sensitive (e.g., Abbott 1994; Cable and Gould 1988; Crown 1981; Deaver 1990; Henderson 1995:106–109; Newman and Woodson 2002).

The next step is to analyze a larger portion of the middle Gila survey data. One particularly promising candidate for future research is the area surrounding the site of Sweetwater (GR-931), where Woodson (2002) notes that many surface assemblages lack prehistoric diagnostic sherds, commercial historic materials (e.g., metal, glass, rubber, plastic), and Black-on-red pottery that postdates the mid-1800s. He suggests that some of the activity loci marked by these assemblages may represent Protohistoric deposits. However, these assemblages may signal functional, rather than temporal, differences. Another site is GR-453, an Historic (about A.D. 1880 to 1920) *ki* (pit house) in the Borderlands region of the

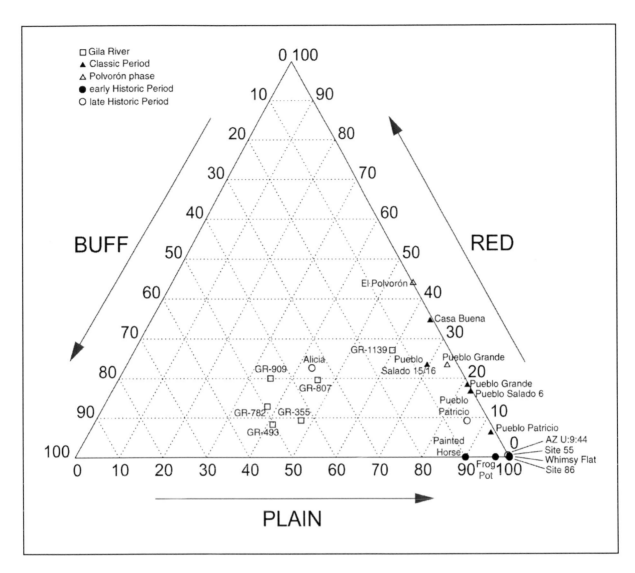

Figure 10. Trivariate plot of the ceramic frequency data in Table 5, with Plain, Buff, and Red ware variables as axes.

Gila River Indian Community (Bubemyer et al. 1998:26–28). Survey of this site yielded a wire-wrap wound glass bead, manufactured in China between the 1400s and 1650s (Francis 2002).

Once sites in the middle Gila survey region have been identified as candidates for further investigation, then more detailed analyses of their late Classic and early Historic pottery need to be undertaken with the principal objective of developing recognizable diagnostic attributes (i.e., surface finish and paste type) of Protohistoric ceramics (see Abbott 1994; Henderson 1995; Whittlesey 1982). More detailed studies of projectile points and their distribution also have the potential to contribute to the development of a diagnostic set of material traits for the Protohistoric (e.g., Loendorf and Rice 2004). The results of these studies then need to be evaluated by testing the sites in the field. The first stage of field testing should involve excavation, with the aim of studying the relationship between microstratigraphy and artifact assemblages, to be followed by more intensive excavations if Protohistoric materials are confirmed in these investigations.

Finally, direct and continuous involvement of modern Akimel O'odham and Pee Posh members of the Gila River Indian Community is required to aid in interpreting documentary sources and in recording personal narratives that can inform about aspects of modern and historical settlement and land use practices, which potentially could lead to more reliable means for identifying Protohistoric sites. Wilson's (1999) recent efforts are evidence that this approach is intellectually profitable for understanding Pima history and process along the middle Gila.

REFERENCES CITED

Abbott, D. R.
  1994   *The Pueblo Grande Project: Ceramics and the Production and Exchange of Pottery in the Central Phoenix Basin.* Publications in Archaeology No. 20. Soil Systems, Phoenix, Arizona.

  2000   *Ceramics and Community Organization among the Hohokam.* University of Arizona Press, Tucson.

Abbott, D. R. (editor)
  2003   *Centuries of Decline during the Hohokam Classic Period at Pueblo Grande.* University of Arizona Press, Tucson.

Abbott, D. R., D. R. Mitchell, and J. A. Merewether
  1994   Chronology. In *The Pueblo Grande Project: Feature Descriptions, Chronology, and Site Structure,* edited by D. R. Mitchell, pp. 6.1–6.197. Publications in Archaeology No. 20. Soil Systems, Phoenix, Arizona.

Adams, E. C., M. T. Stark, and D. S. Dosh
  1993   Ceramic Distribution and Exchange: Jeddito Yellow Ware and Implications for Social Complexity. *Journal of Field Archaeology* 20(1):3–21.

Adams, E. C., and A. I. Duff (editors)
  2004   *The Protohistoric Pueblo World, A.D. 1275–1600.* University of Arizona Press, Tucson.

Ahlstrom, R. V. N., M. L. Chenault, M. Zyniecki, and D. H. Greenwald
  1995   Chronology, Compound Growth, and Demography. In *Early Desert Farming and Irrigation Settlements: Archaeological Investigations in the Phoenix Sky Harbor Center: Pueblo Salado,* edited by D. H. Greenwald, M. L. Chenault, and D. M. Greenwald, pp. 369–394. Anthropological Research Paper No. 4. SWCA, Flagstaff, Arizona.

Andresen, J. M.
  1985   Pottery and Architecture at Compound F, Casa Grande Ruins National Monument, Arizona. In *Proceedings of the 1983 Hohokam Symposium Part II,* edited by A. E. Dittert and D. E. Dove, pp. 595–630. Occasional Paper No. 2. Arizona Archaeological Society, Phoenix.

Ayres, J. E.
  1971   An Early Historic Burial from the Village of Bac. *The Kiva* 36(2):44–48.

Barnes, M. R.
  1984   Hispanic Period Archaeology in the Tucson Basin: An Overview. *The Kiva* 49(3–4):213–223.

Bayman, J. M.
  2001   The Hohokam of Southwest North America. *Journal of World Prehistory* 15(3):257–311.

Bayman, J. M., and R. M. Ryan
1988   Lower Colorado Buffware and the Protohistoric Period in Southern Arizona. *Pottery Southwest* 15(1).

Becker, K. M., and J. H. Altschul
2003   *Historic Context for Prehistoric and Protohistoric Trails and Related Features at Yuma Proving Ground, Arizona.* Technical Report No. 03–13. Statistical Research, Tucson, Arizona.

Beckwith, K. E.
1986   Artifacts of Local Manufacture—Ceramics. In *Archaeological Investigations at AZ U:14:75(ASM), A Turn of the Century Pima Homestead,* edited by R. W. Layhe, pp. 59–78. Archaeological Series No. 172. Arizona State Museum, University of Arizona, Tucson.

Bertelsen, R.
1988   The Finds Pattern of Archaeological Excavation: Correspondence Analysis as Explorative Tool. In *Computer and Quantitative Methods in Archaeology, 1987,* edited by C. L. N. Ruggles and S. P. Q. Rahtz, pp. 25–28. International Series No. 393. British Archaeological Reports, Oxford.

Betancourt, J. L.
1978   *An Archaeological Synthesis of the Tucson Basin: Focus on Santa Cruz and its Riverpark.* Archaeological Series No. 116. Arizona State Museum, University of Arizona, Tucson.

Bolton, H. E.
1919   *Kino's Historical Memoir of Pimería Alta,* vol. 1. The Arthur H. Clark Company, Cleveland, Ohio.

1930   *Anza's California Expeditions,* vols. I–V. University of California Press, Berkeley.

1948   *Kino's Historical Memoir of Pimería Alta: A Contemporary Account of the Beginnings of California, Sonora, and Arizona, by Father Eusebio Francisco Kino, S. J. Pioneer Missionary, Explorer, Cartographer, and Ranchman, 1683–1711.* University of California Press, Berkeley.

Bølviken, E., E. Helskog, K. Helskog, I. M. Holm-Olsen, L. Solheim, and R. Bertelsen
1982   Correspondence Analysis: An Alternative to Principal Components. *World Archaeology* 1(1):(41–60).

Bostwick, T. W., and C. E. Downum (editors)
1994   *Archaeology of the Pueblo Grande Platform Mound and Surrounding Features, Volume 2: Features in the Central Precinct of the Pueblo Grande Community.* Anthropological Papers No. 1. Pueblo Grande Museum, Phoenix, Arizona.

Bostwick, T. W., D. H. Greenwald, and M.-E. Walsh-Anduze
1996   *Exploring the Hohokam to Pima Transition in the Salt River Valley.* Paper presented at the 1995 Fall Conference of the Arizona Archaeological Council, Flagstaff.

Brainerd, G. W.
1951 The Place of Chronological Ordering in Archaeological Analysis. *American Antiquity* 16(3):301–313.

Brew, S. A., and B. B. Huckell
1987 A Protohistoric Piman Burial and a Consideration of Piman Burial Practices. *The Kiva* 52(3):163–191.

Bronitsky, G.
1985 The Protohistoric Pimans of Southeastern Arizona: A Review of History, Archaeology, and Material Culture. In *Southwestern Culture History: Collected Papers in Honor of Albert H. Schroeder,* edited by C. H. Lange, pp. 139–151. Papers of the Archaeological Society of New Mexico, Vol. 10. Ancient City Press, Santa Fe, New Mexico.

Bronitsky, G., and J. D. Merritt
1986 *The Archaeology of Southeast Arizona: A Class 1 Cultural Resource Inventory.* Bureau of Land Management, Phoenix, Arizona.

Bruder, J. S.
1975 Historic Papago Archaeology. In *Hecla II and III: An Interpretive Study of Archaeological Remains from the Lakeshore Project, Papago Reservation, South Central Arizona,* edited by A. C. Goodyear, pp. 271–337. Anthropological Research Papers No. 9. Arizona State University, Tempe.

Bubemyer, T., M. Brodbeck, and R. B. Neily
1998 *A Cultural Resources Survey of the Borderlands Area, Gila River Indian Community, Maricopa County, Arizona.* CRMP Technical Report 1997-23. Cultural Resource Management Program, Gila River Indian Community, Sacaton, Arizona.

Burrus, E. J.
1971 *Kino and Manje: Explorers of Sonora and Arizona.* Sources and Studies for the History of the Americas X. Jesuit Historical Institute, Rome.

Cable, J. S.
1990 Who Were the Protohistoric Occupants of Ak-Chin? A Study Concerning the Relationship Between Ethnicity and Ceramic Style. In *Archaeology of the Ak-Chin Indian Community West Side Farms Project: Subsistence Studies and Synthesis and Interpretation,* edited by R. E. Gasser, R. K. Robinson, and C. D. Breternitz, pp. 23.1–23.65. Publications in Archaeology No. 9. Soil Systems, Phoenix, Arizona.

Cable, J. S., and R. R. Gould
1988 The Casa Buena Ceramic Assemblage: A Study of Typological Systematics and Ceramic Change in Classic Period Assemblages. In *Excavations at Casa Buena: Changing Hohokam Land Use along Squaw Peak Parkway,* edited by J. B. Howard, pp. 271–357. Publications in Archaeology No. 11. Soil Systems, Phoenix, Arizona.

Cable, J. S., and D. R. Mitchell
  1988 La Lomita Pequeña in Regional Perspective. In *Excavations at La Lomita Pequeña: A Santa Cruz/Sacaton Phase Hamlet in the Salt River Valley,* edited by D. R. Mitchell, pp. 395–446. Publications in Archaeology No. 10. Soil Systems, Phoenix, Arizona.

Castetter, E. F., and W. H. Bell
  1942 *Pima & Papago Indian Agriculture.* University of New Mexico Press, Albuquerque.

Caywood, L. R.
  1950 Hispanic Pottery as a Guide in Historical Studies. In *For the Dean: Essays in Anthropology in Honor of Byron Cummings on His Eighty-ninth Birthday, September 20, 1950,* edited by E. K. Reed and D. S. King, pp. 77–97. Hohokam Museums Association, Tucson, Arizona.

Chase, P. G.
  1985 Whole Vessels and Sherds: An Experimental Investigation of Their Quantitative Relationship. *Journal of Field Archaeology* 12(2):213–218.

Cheek, A. L.
  1974 *The Evidence for Acculturation in Artifacts: Indians and Non-Indians at San Xavier del Bac, Arizona.* Unpublished Ph.D. dissertation, Department of Anthropology, University of Arizona, Tucson.

Chenault, M. L.
  1993 The Hohokam Post-Classic Polvorón Phase. In *Early Desert Farming and Irrigation Settlements: Archaeological Investigations in the Phoenix Sky Harbor Center, Volume 4: Special Studies, Synthesis and Conclusions,* edited by D. H. Greenwald and J. H. Ballagh, pp. 117–140. Archaeological Report No. 93-17. SWCA, Flagstaff, Arizona.

  1996 *The Polvorón Phase and the Hohokam Collapse.* Unpublished Ph.D. dissertation, Department of Anthropology, University of Colorado, Boulder.

  2000 In Defense of the Polvorón Phase. In *The Hohokam Village Revisited,* edited by D. E. Doyel, S. K. Fish, and P. R. Fish, pp. 277–286. American Association for the Advancement of Science, Fort Collins, Colorado.

Clark, J. J.
  2001 *Tracking Prehistoric Migrations: Pueblo Settlers among the Tonto Basin Hohokam.* Anthropological Papers No. 65. University of Arizona Press, Tucson.

Clouse, R. A.
  1999 Interpreting Archaeological Data through Correspondence Analysis. *Historical Archaeology* 33(2):90–107.

Colton, H. S.
1956 *Pottery Types of the Southwest: Tsegi Orange Ware, Winslow Orange Ware, Homolovi Orange Ware, Jeddito Yellow Ware, Awatovi Yellow Ware.* Ceramic Series 3C. Museum of Northern Arizona, Flagstaff.

1958 *Pottery Types of the Southwest: Wares 14, 15, 16, 17: Alameda Brown Ware, Lower Colorado Buff Ware, Prescott Gray Ware, San Francisco Mountain Gray Ware.* Ceramic Series 3D. Museum of Northern Arizona, Flagstaff.

Cordell, L. S.
1984 *Prehistory of the Southwest.* Academic Press, Orlando, Florida.

Cowgill, G. L.
1964 The Selection of Samples from Large Sherd Collections. *American Antiquity* 29(4):467–473.

1990 Why Pearson's *r* Is Not a Good Similarity Coefficient for Comparing Collections. *American Antiquity* 55(4):512–521.

Crown, P. L.
1981 Analysis of Las Colinas Ceramics. In *The 1968 Excavations at Mound 8, Las Colinas Ruins Group, Phoenix, Arizona,* edited by L. C. Hammack and A. P. Sullivan, pp. 87–169. Archaeological Series No. 154. Arizona State Museum, University of Arizona, Tucson.

1983 Intrusive Ceramics and the Identification of Hohokam Exchange Networks. In *Proceedings of the 1983 Hohokam Symposium, Part II*, edited by A. E. Dittert and D. E. Dove, pp. 439–458. Occasional Paper No. 2. Arizona Archaeological Society, Phoenix.

1984 Ceramic Vessel Exchange in Southern Arizona. In *Hohokam Archaeology along the Salt-Gila Aqueduct: Synthesis and Conclusions,* edited by L. S. Teague and P. L. Crown, pp. 251–303. Archaeological Series No. 150. Arizona State Museum, University of Arizona, Tucson.

1994 *Ceramics and Ideology: Salado Polychrome Pottery.* University of New Mexico Press, Albuquerque.

Crown, P. L., and E. W. Sires
1984 The Hohokam Chronology and Salt-Gila Aqueduct Project Research. In *Hohokam Archaeology along the Salt-Gila Aqueduct: Synthesis and Conclusions,* edited by L. S. Teague and P. L. Crown, pp. 73–85. Archaeological Series No. 150. Arizona State Museum, University of Arizona, Tucson.

Danson, E., and R. Wallace
1956 A Petrographic Study of Gila Polychrome. *American Antiquity* 22(2):180–183.

Darling, J. A., J. C. Ravesloot, and M. R. Waters
2004   Village Drift and Riverine Settlement: Modeling Akimel O'odham Land Use. *American Anthropologist* 106(2):282–295.

Dart, A.
1994   *Archaeological Studies of the Avra Valley, Arizona: Excavations in the Schuk Toak District.* Anthropological Papers No. 16. Center for Desert Archaeology, Tucson, Arizona.

Dean, J. S.
1991   Thoughts on Hohokam Chronology. In *Exploring the Hohokam: Prehistoric Desert Peoples of the American Southwest,* edited by G. J. Gumerman, pp. 61–149. University of New Mexico Press, Albuquerque.

Deaver, W. L.
1989   Southwestern Archaeomagnetic Secular Variation: The Hohokam Data. In *The 1982–1984 Excavations at Las Colinas: Syntheses and Conclusions,* edited by L. S. Teague and W. L. Deaver, pp. 7–41. Archaeological Series No. 162. Arizona State Museum, University of Arizona, Tucson.

1990   Native American Ceramics. In *Archaeology of the Ak-Chin Indian Community West Side Farms Project: Material Culture and Human Remains,* edited by R. E. Gasser, C. K. Robinson, and C. D. Breternitz, pp. 15.1–15.35. Publications in Archaeology No. 9. Soil Systems, Phoenix, Arizona.

Di Peso, C. C.
1951   *The Babocomari Village Site on the Babocomari River, Southeastern Arizona.* Publication No. 5. Amerind Foundation, Dragoon, Arizona.

1953   *The Sobaipuri Indians of the Upper San Pedro River Valley.* Publication No. 6. Amerind Foundation, Dragoon, Arizona.

1956   *The Upper Pima of San Cayetano del Tumacacori: An Archaeohistorical Reconstruction of the O'otam of the Pimería Alta.* Publication No. 7. Amerind Foundation, Dragoon, Arizona.

1958   *The Reeve Ruin of Southeastern Arizona: A Study of a Prehistoric Western Pueblo Migration into the Middle San Pedro Valley.* Publication No. 8. Amerind Foundation, Dragoon, Arizona.

1974   *Casas Grandes: A Fallen Trading Center of the Gran Chichimeca, Volumes 1–3* Publication No. 9(1–3). Amerind Foundation, Dragoon, Arizona.

1981   Discussion of Masse, Doelle, Sheridan, and Reff Papers from Southwestern Protohistory Conference. In *The Protohistoric Period in the North American Southwest, AD 1450–1700,* edited by D. R. Wilcox and W. B. Masse, pp. 113–128. Anthropological Research Papers No. 24. Arizona State University, Tempe.

Dittert, A. E., and F. Plog
  1980   *Generations in Clay.* Northland Press, Flagstaff, Arizona.

Dobyns, H. F.
  1963   Indian Extinction in the Middle Santa Cruz River Valley, Arizona. *New Mexico Historical Review* 38:163–181.

Dobyns, H. F., and R. C. Euler
  1958   Tizon Brown Ware: A Descriptive Revision. In *Pottery Types of the Southwest*, edited by H. S. Colton. Ceramic Series 30. Museum of Northern Arizona, Flagstaff.

Doelle, W. H.
  1981   The Gila Pima in the Late Seventeenth Century. In *The Protohistoric Period in the North American Southwest, AD 1450–1700,* edited by D. R. Wilcox and W. B. Masse, pp. 57–70. Anthropological Research Papers 24. Department of Anthropology, Arizona State University, Tempe.

  1984   The Tucson Basin During the Protohistoric Period. *The Kiva* 49(3–4):195–211.

  1995   Regional Platform Mound Systems: Background and Inventory. In *The Roosevelt Community Development Study: New Perspectives on Tonto Basin Prehistory,* edited by M. D. Elson, M. T. Stark, and D. A. Gregory, pp. 555–560. Anthropological Papers No. 15. Center for Desert Archaeology, Tucson, Arizona.

Doelle, W. H., D. A. Gregory, and H. D. Wallace
  1995   Classic Period Platform Mound Systems in Southern Arizona. In *The Roosevelt Community Development Study,* edited by M. D. Elson, M. T. Stark, and D. A. Gregory, pp. 385–440. Anthropological Papers No. 15. Center for Desert Archaeology, Tucson, Arizona.

Doelle, W. H., and H. D. Wallace
  1990   The Transition to History in the Pimería Alta. In *Perspectives on Southwestern Prehistory,* edited by P. E. Minnis and C. L. Redman, pp. 239–257. Westview Press, Boulder, Colorado.

Doran, J. E., and F. R. Hodson
  1975   *Mathematics and Computers in Archaeology.* Harvard University Press, Cambridge, Massachusetts.

Douglas, F. H.
  1953   Five Pima Pots. In *Material Culture Notes* 18:83–86. Denver Art Museum, Denver, Colorado.

Downum, C. E.
  1993   *Between Desert and River: Hohokam Settlement and Land Use in the Los Robles Community.* Anthropological Papers No. 57. University of Arizona Press, Tucson.

Downum, C. E., A. G. Rankin, and J. S. Czaplicki
1986 *A Class III Archaeological Survey of the Phase B Corridor, Tucson Aqueduct, CAP. Late Archaic; Late Pioneer, Colonial, Sedentary, and Early Classic Period Tucson Basin Hohokam; & Sobaipuri Occupation in the Avra Valley, Southern AZ.* Archaeological Series 168. Arizona State Museum, University of Arizona, Tucson.

Doyel, D. E.
1974 *Excavations in the Escalante Ruin Group, Southern Arizona.* Archaeological Series No. 37. Arizona State Museum, University of Arizona, Tucson.

1977 *Excavations in the Middle Santa Cruz River Valley, Southeastern Arizona.* Contributions to Highway Salvage Archaeology in Arizona No. 44. Arizona State Museum, University of Arizona, Tucson.

1980 Hohokam Social Organization and the Sedentary to Classic Tradition. In *Current Issues in Hohokam Prehistory,* edited by F. Plog, pp. 23–40. Anthropological Research Papers No. 23. Department of Anthropology, Arizona State University, Tempe.

1981 *Late Hohokam Prehistory in Southern Arizona.* Contributions to Archaeology No. 2. Gila Press, Scottsdale, Arizona.

1991 Hohokam Cultural Evolution in the Phoenix Basin. In *Exploring the Hohokam: Prehistoric Desert People of the American Southwest,* edited by G. J. Gumerman, pp. 231–278. University of New Mexico Press, Albuquerque.

1995 A Regional Perspective on the Late Classic Period in the Phoenix Basin. In *Archaeological Investigations at Pueblo Blanco: The MCDOT Alma School Road Project,* edited by D. E. Doyel, A. T. Black, and B. S. Macnider, pp. 483–495. Archaeological Resources Report No. 90. Archaeological Consulting Services, Tempe, Arizona.

Doyel, D. E., and M. Green
1995 *Research Design and Work Plan for Archaeological Survey of the Gila River Indian Community.* Unpublished ACS Report. Archaeological Consulting Services, Tempe, Arizona.

Drucker, P.
1941 *Cultural Element Distributions, XVII: Yuman-Piman.* Anthropological Records No. 6. University of California Press, Berkeley.

Duff, A. I.
2002 *Western Pueblo Identities: Regional Interaction, Migration, and Transformation.* University of Arizona Press, Tucson.

Duffen, W., and Hartmann, W. K.
1997 The 76 Ranch Ruin and the Location of Chichilticale. In *The Coronado Expedition to Tierra Nueva: The 1540–1542 Route across the Southwest,* edited by R. Flint and S. Cushing Flint. University Press of Colorado, Niwot.

Dunne, P. M.
 1955 *Jacobo Sedelmayr: Missionary, Frontiersman, Explorer in Arizona and Sonora; Four Original Manuscript Narratives, 1744–1751.* Arizona Pioneers' Historical Society, Tucson.

Dunnell, R. C., and W. S. Dancey
 1983 The Siteless Survey: A Regional Scale Data Collection Strategy. In *Advances in Archaeological Method and Theory*, edited by M. B. Schiffer, vol. 6, pp. 267–287. Academic Press, New York.

Dykeman, D. D., R. H. Towner, and J. K. Feathers
 2002 Correspondence in Tree-Ring and Thermoluminescence Dating: A Protohistoric Navajo Pilot Study. *American Antiquity* 67:145–164.

Eighmy, J. L., and D. E. Doyel
 1987 A Re-analysis of First Reported Archaeomagnetic Dates from the Hohokam Area, Southern Arizona. *Journal of Field Archaeology* 14(3):331–342.

Eighmy, J. L., and J. H. Hathaway
 1987 Contemporary Archaeomagnetic Results and the Accuracy of Archaeomagnetic Dates. *Geoarchaeology* 2(1):41–61.

Eighmy, J. L., and R. H. McGuire
 1989 Dating the Hohokam Phase Sequence: An Analysis of Archaeomagnetic Dates. *Journal of Field Archaeology* 16(1):15–31.

Eiselt, B. S., M. K. Woodson, J. Touchin, and E. Davis
 2002 *A Cultural Resources Assessment of the Casa Blanca Management Area, Pima Maricopa Irrigation Project (P-MIP), Gila River Indian Community, Arizona.* P-MIP Report No. 8. Cultural Resource Management Program, Gila River Indian Community, Sacaton, Arizona.

Elson, M. D.
 1998 *Expanding the View of Hohokam Platform Mounds: An Ethnographic Perspective.* Anthropological Papers No. 63. University of Arizona Press, Tucson.

Elson, M. D., and D. R. Abbott
 2000 Organizational Variability in Platform Mound-building Groups of the American Southwest. In *Alternative Leadership Strategies in the Prehispanic Southwest,* edited by B. L. Mills, pp. 117–135. University of Arizona Press, Tucson.

Euler, R. T.
 1987 Flaked Stone Assemblage. In *The Archaeology of the San Xavier Bridge Site (AZ BB:13:14), Tucson Basin, Southern Arizona, Parts 1 and 2,* edited by J. C. Ravesloot, pp. 227–238. Archaeological Series No. 171. Arizona State Museum, University of Arizona, Tucson.

Ezell, P. H.
1957   The Conditions of Hispanic-Piman Contacts on the Gila River. *América Indígena* 17(2):163–191.

1961   The Hispanic Acculturation of the Gila River Pimas. *American Anthropologist* 63(5):Part 2, Memoir 90 of the American Anthropological Association.

1963   Is There a Hohokam-Pima Culture Continuum? *American Antiquity* 29(1):61–65.

1983   History of the Pima. In *Southwest,* edited by A. Ortiz, pp. 149–160. *Handbook of North American Indians,* vol. 10. Smithsonian Institution, Washington, D.C.

Feathers, J. K.
1997   The Application of Luminescence Dating in American Archaeology. *Journal of Archaeological Method and Theory* 4:1–67.

2000   Date List 7: Luminescence Dates for Prehistoric and Proto-Historic Pottery from the American Southwest. *Ancient TL* 18:51–61.

2002   Thermoluminescence Dating of Pottery Sherds from the Sweetwater Site, Gila River Indian Community, Arizona. In *Archaeological Investigations at the Sweetwater Site along State Route 587 on the Gila River Indian Community,* edited by M. K. Woodson, pp. 274–278. P-MIP Technical Report No. 2002-14. Cultural Resources Management Program, Gila River Indian Community, Sacaton, Arizona.

Fink, T. M.
1991   Paleonutrition and Paleopathology of the Salt River Hohokam: A Search for Correlates. *Kiva* 56(2):293–318.

Fish, P. R.
1989   The Hohokam: 1,000 Years of Prehistory in the Sonoran Desert. In *Dynamics of Southwest Prehistory,* edited by L. S. Cordell and G. J. Gumerman, pp. 19–63. Smithsonian Institution Press, Washington, D.C.

Fish, S. K., and P. R. Fish
1994   An Assessment of Abandonment Processes in the Hohokam Classic Period of the Tucson Basin. In *Ethnoarchaeological and Archaeological Approaches,* edited by C. M. Cameron and S. A. Tomka, pp. 99–109. Cambridge University Press, Cambridge.

Fish, S. K., P. R. Fish, and J. H. Madsen (editors)
1992   *The Marana Community in the Hohokam World.* Anthropological Papers No. 56. University of Arizona Press, Tucson.

Fontana, B. L.
1965   On the Meaning of Historic Sites Archaeology. *American Antiquity* 31(1):61–65.

Fontana B. L., and D. S. Matson
  1987   Santa Ana de Cuiquiburitac: Pimería Alta's Northernmost Mission. *Journal of the Southwest* 29:133–159.

Fontana, B. L., W. J. Robinson, C. W. Cormack, and E. E. Leavitt
  1962   *Papago Indian Pottery.* University of Washington Press, Seattle.

Foster, M. S.
  1994   *The Pueblo Grande Project: Volume 1: Introduction, Research Design, and Testing Results.* Soil Systems, Phoenix, Arizona.

Fowler, A. P.
  1989   *Ceramic Types of the Zuni Area.* New Mexico Archaeological Council Ceramics Workshop, Silver City.

Francis, P.
  2002   *Asia's Maritime Bead Trade from ca. 300 BC to the Present.* University of Hawai'i Press, Honolulu.

Franklin, H. H.
  1980   *Excavations at Second Canyon Ruin, San Pedro Valley, Arizona.* Unpublished manuscript, on file with the Arizona State Museum, University of Arizona, Tucson.

Fritz, G. L.
  1989   The Ecological Significance of Early Piman Immigration to Southern Arizona. *The Artifact* 27(1):51–110.

Garrett, B. G., and S. C. Russell
  1983   A Model for the Household Complex of the Gila Pima: 1853–1920. In *Alicia: The History of a Piman Homestead*, edited by G. E. Rice, S. Upham, and L. Nicholas, pp. 11–36. Anthropological Field Studies No. 4. Office of Cultural Resource Management, Arizona State University, Tempe.

Gasser, R. E.
  1990   Ak-Chin Farming. In *Archaeology of the Ak-Chin Indian Community West Side Farms Project: The Land and the People*[AE1], [CW2]edited by R. E. Gasser, C. K. Robinson, and C. D. Breternitz, pp. 4.1–4.29. Soil Systems, Phoenix, Arizona.

Gasser, R. E., C. K. Robinson, and D. C. Breternitz
  1990   *Archaeology of the Ak-Chin Indian Community West Side Farms Project: The Land and the People, Volume II.* Soil Systems, Phoenix, Arizona.

Gerald, R. E.
  1968   *Spanish Presidios of the Late Eighteenth Century in Northern New Spain.* Museum of New Mexico Press, Albuquerque.

Gilpin, D., and D. A. Phillips
  1998 *The Prehistoric to Historic Transition Period in Arizona, Circa A.D. 1519 to 1692.* Report Submitted to the Arizona State Historic Preservation Office, Arizona State Parks Board, Phoenix.

Gladwin, H. S., E. W. Haury, E. B. Sayles, and N. Gladwin
  1937 *Excavations at Snaketown: Material Culture.* Medallion Papers No. 25. Gila Pueblo, Globe, Arizona.

Gladwin, W., and H. S. Gladwin
  1935 *The Eastern Range of the Red-on-Buff Culture.* Medallion Papers No. 16. Gila Pueblo, Globe, Arizona.

Goodyear, A. C.
  1977 The Historical and Ecological Position of Protohistoric Sites in the Slate Mountains, South-Central Arizona. In *Research Strategies in Historical Archaeology,* edited by S. South, pp. 203–239. Academic Press, New York.

Graybill, D. A., D. A. Gregory, G. S. Funkhouser, and F. L. Nials
  1999 Long-Term Streamflow Reconstructions, River Channel Morphology, and Aboriginal Irrigation Systems along the Salt and Gila Rivers. In *Environmental Change and Human Adaptation in the Ancient Southwest,* edited by J. S. Dean and D. E. Doyel. University of Utah Press, Salt Lake City.

Graybill, D. A., and F. L. Nials
  1989 Aspects of Climate, Streamflow, and Geomorphology Affecting Irrigation Systems in the Salt River Valley. In *The 1982–1984 Excavations at Las Colinas: Environment and Subsistence,* edited by C. A. Heathington and D. A. Gregory, pp. 39–58. Archaeological Series No. 162. Arizona State Museum, University of Arizona, Tucson.

Grebinger, P. F.
  1976 The Salado: Perspectives from the Middle Santa Cruz Valley. *The Kiva* 42(11):39–46.

Greenacre, M.
  1994 Correspondence Analysis and Its Interpretation. In *Correspondence Analysis in the Social Sciences,* edited by M. Greenacre and J. Blasius, pp. 3–22. Academic Press, New York.

Greenwald, D. H., and J. H. Ballagh (editors)
  1993 *Early Desert Farming: Archaeological Investigations in the Phoenix Sky Harbor Center: Special Studies, Synthesis, and Conclusions.* Anthropological Research Paper No. 17. SWCA, Flagstaff.

Greenwald, D. H., J. H. Ballagh, D. R. Mitchell, and R. A. Anduze (editors)
  1996 *Life on the Floodplain: Further Investigations at Pueblo Salado for Phoenix Sky Harbor International Airport, Volume 2, Data Recovery and Re-evaluation, Part 1: The Report.* Anthropological Papers No. 4. Pueblo Grande Museum, Phoenix.

Greenwald, D. H., and R. Ciolek-Torello
1988   *Archaeological Excavations at the Dutch Canal Ruin, Phoenix, Arizona.* Research Paper No. 38. Museum of Northern Arizona, Flagstaff.

Gregory, D. A.
1987   The Morphology of Platform Mounds and the Structure of Classic Period Hohokam Sites. In *The Hohokam Village: Site Organization and Structure,* edited by D. E. Doyel, pp. 183–210. American Association for the Advancement of Science, Glenwood Springs, Colorado.

1988   The Changing Spatial Structure of the Mound 8 Precinct. In *1982–1984 Excavations at Las Colinas: The Mound 8 Precinct,* edited by D. A. Gregory, pp. 25–50. Archaeological Series No. 164. Arizona State Museum, University of Arizona, Tucson.

1991   Form and Variation in Hohokam Settlement Patterns. In *Chaco and Hohokam: Prehistoric Regional Systems in the American Southwest,* edited by P. L. Crown and W. J. Judge, pp. 159–194. School of American Research Press, Santa Fe, New Mexico.

Gregory, D. A., and F. L. Nials
1985   Observations Concerning the Distribution of Classic Period Hohokam Platform Mounds. In *Proceedings of the 1983 Hohokam Symposium,* edited by A. E. Dittert and D. E. Dove, pp. 373–388. Occasional Paper No. 2. Arizona Archaeological Society, Phoenix.

Gumerman, G. J. (editor)
1991   *Exploring the Hohokam: Prehistoric Desert Peoples of the American Southwest,* University of New Mexico Press, Albuquerque.

1994   *Themes in Southwest Prehistory.* School of American Research Press, Santa Fe, New Mexico.

Hackbarth, M. R.
1995   Integration of the MTS Data with the Late Classic Period Hohokam. In *Archaeology at the Head of the Scottsdale Canal System, Volume 3: Case Studies and Synthesis,* edited by M. R. Hackbarth, T. K. Henderson, and D. B. Craig, pp. 173–195. Anthropological Papers No. 95–1. Northland Research, Flagstaff, Arizona.

Hackenberg, R. A.
1983   Pima and Papago Ecological Adaptations. In *Handbook of North American Indians,* vol. 10, *edited by* pp. 161–177. Smithsonian Institution, Washington, D.C.

Hallenbeck, C.
1940   *Alvar Nunez Cabeza de Vaca: The Journey and Route of the First European to Cross the Continent of North America.* Arthur H. Clark, Glendale, California.

Hammack, L. C., and A. P. Sullivan
1981   *The 1968 Excavations at Mound 8 Las Colinas Ruins Group, Phoenix, Arizona.* Arizona State Museum, University of Arizona, Tucson.

62

Hammond, G. P., and A. Rey
1940 *Narratives of the Coronado Expedition, 1540–1542.* University of New Mexico Press, Albuquerque.

Harwell, H. O., and M. C. S. Kelly
1983 Maricopa. In *Southwest*, edited by A. Ortiz, pp. 71–85. *Handbook of North American Indians,* vol. 10. Smithsonian Institution, Washington, D.C.

Haury, E. W.
1945 *The Excavation of Los Muertos and Neighboring Ruins in the Salt River Valley, Southern Arizona.* Peabody Museum, Harvard University, Cambridge, Massachusetts.

1958 Evidence at Point of Pines for a Prehistoric Migration from Northern Arizona. In *Migrations in New World Culture History*, edited by R. H. Thompson, pp. 1–8. University of Arizona Press, Tucson.

1976 *The Hohokam: Desert Farmers and Craftsmen: Excavations at Snaketown, 1964–1965.* University of Arizona Press, Tucson.

1984 The Search for Chichilticale. *Arizona Highways* 60(4):14–19.

Haury, E. W., K. Bryan, E. H. Colbert, N. Gabel, C. L. Tanner, and T. E. Buehrer
1950 *The Stratigraphy and Archaeology of Ventana Cave, Arizona.* University of Arizona Press, Tucson.

Hayden, J. D.
1957 *Excavations, 1940, at the University Indian Ruin.* Southwestern Monuments Association Technical Series No. 154. University of Arizona, Tucson.

1959 Notes on Pima Pottery Making. *The Kiva* 24(3):10–16.

Heidke, J., and M. D. Elson
1988 Tucson Basin Stucco-Coated Plain Ware: A Technological Assessment. *The Kiva* 53:273–285.

Henderson, T. K.
1995 *The Prehistoric Archaeology of Heritage Square.* Anthropological Papers No. 3. Pueblo Grande Museum, Phoenix, Arizona.

Henderson, T. K., and M. R. Hackbarth
2000 What is Going on at the Hohokam Village? A Fourteenth and Fifteenth Century Perspective. In *The Hohokam Village Revisited,* edited by D. E. Doyel, S. K. Fish, and P. R. Fish, pp. 287–316. American Association for the Advancement of Science, Fort Collins, Colorado.

Henderson, T. K., and R. J. Martynec (editors)
1993   *Classic Period Occupation on the Santa Cruz Flats: The Santa Cruz Flats Archaeological Project.* Northland Research, Flagstaff, Arizona.

Howard, J. B.
1987   The Lehi Canal System: Organization of a Classic Period Community. In *The Hohokam Village: Site Structure and Organization,* edited by D. E. Doyel, pp. 211–221. American Association for the Advancement of Science, Glenwood Springs, Colorado.

Howard, J. B. (editor)
1988   *Excavations at Casa Buena: Changing Hohokam Land Use along the Squaw Peak Parkway.* Publications in Archaeology No. 11. Soil Systems, Phoenix, Arizona.

Howell, T. L.
1993   *Archaeological Investigations at Los Guanacos: Exploring Cultural Changes in Late Hohokam Society.* Northland Research, Flagstaff, Arizona.

Hrdlička, A.
1906   Notes on the Pima of Arizona. *American Anthropologist* 8(1):39–46.

Huckell, B. B.
1980   Results of Testing: Protohistoric Period Sites. In *ANAMAX-Rosemont Testing Project,* edited by B. B. Huckell, pp. 137–159. Arizona State Museum, University of Arizona, Tucson.

1984   Sobaipuri Sites in the Rosemont Area. In *Miscellaneous Archaeological Studies in the ANAMAX-Rosemont Land Exchange Area,* edited by M. D. Tagg, R. G. Ervin, and B. B. Huckell, pp. 107–146. Archaeological Series No. 171. Arizona State Museum, University of Arizona, Tucson.

Huckell, L. W.
1981   *Archaeological Test Excavations at the U.S. Home Corporation, Saddlewood Ranch Proposed Development Area.* Arizona State Museum, University of Arizona, Tucson.

Huckleberry, G.
1999   Stratigraphic Identification of Destructive Floods in Relict Canals: A Case Study from the Middle Gila River, Arizona. *Kiva* 65(1):7–35

Justice, N. D.
2002   *Stone Age Spear and Arrow Points of the Southwestern United States.* Indiana University Press, Bloomington.

Karns, H. J. (translator)
1954   *Unknown Arizona and Sonora.* Desert Silhouettes, Tucson, Arizona.

Kent, S.

1992 Studying Variability in the Archaeological Record: An Ethnoarchaeological Model for Distinguishing Mobility Patterns. *American Antiquity* 57: 635–660.

Kintigh, K. W.

1985 Social Structure, the Structure of Style, and Stylistic Patterns in Cibola Prehistory. In *Decoding Prehistoric Ceramics,* edited by B. A. Nelson, pp. 362–385. Southern Illinois University, Carbondale.

Kisselburg, J. E.

1989 *Investigations at a Pima Household Complex AZ U:14:79 (ASM), Gila River Housing Authority, Sacaton, Arizona, Project AZ 15-32.* Northland Research, Flagstaff, Arizona.

Landis, D. G.

1990 Ak-Chin Lithic Assemblages. In *Archaeology of the Ak-Chin Indian Community West Side Farms Project: Material Culture and Human Remains,* edited by R. E. Gasser, C. K. Robinson, and C. D. Breternitz, pp. 17.1–17.115. Publications in Archaeology No. 12. Soil Systems, Phoenix, Arizona.

Layhe, R. W. (editor)

1986 *Archaeological Investigations at AZ U:14:75(ASM), A Turn of the Century Pima Homestead.* Archaeological Series No. 172. Arizona State Museum, University of Arizona, Tucson.

LeBlanc, S. A.

1999 *Prehistoric Warfare in the American Southwest.* University of Utah Press, Salt Lake City.

Lewarch, D. E., and M. J. O'Brien

1981 The Expanding Role of Surface Assemblages in Archaeological Research. In *Advances in Archaeological Method and Theory*, vol. 4, edited by M. B. Schiffer, pp. 297–342. Academic Press, New York.

Loendorf, C., and G. E. Rice

2004 *Projectile Point Typology: Gila River Indian Community, Arizona.* Anthropological Research Papers No. 2. Cultural Resource Management Program, Gila River Indian Community, Sacaton, Arizona.

Lyman, R. L.

1994 *Vertebrate Taphonomy.* Cambridge University Press, Cambridge.

Lyons, P. D.

2003 *Ancestral Hopi Migrations.* Anthropological Papers No. 68. University of Arizona Press, Tucson.

Majewski, T., and J. E. Ayres
    1997   Toward an Archaeology of Colonialism in the Greater Southwest. *Revista de arqueología americana* 12:55–86.

Marmaduke, W. S., and T. K. Henderson
    1995   *Archaeology in the Distribution Division of the Central Arizona Project.* Northland Research, Flagstaff, Arizona.

Masse, W. B.
    1981   A Reappraisal of the Protohistoric Sobaipuri Indians of Southeastern Arizona. In *The Protohistoric Period in the North American Southwest, AD 1450–1700.,* edited by D. R. Wilcox and W. B. Masse, pp. 28–56. Anthropological Research Papers No. 24. Arizona State University, Tempe.

    1990   Whimsy Flat: AZ T:16:71 (ASM). In *Archaeology of the Ak-Chin Indian Community West Side Farms Project: Subsistence Studies and Synthesis and Interpretation,* edited by R. E. Gasser, C. K. Robinson, and C. D. Breternitz, pp. 12.1–12.37. Soil Systems, Phoenix, Arizona.

Mathien, F. J., and R. H. McGuire (editors)
    1986   *Ripples in the Chichimec Sea: New Considerations of Southwestern-Mesoamerican Interactions.* Southern Illinois University Press, Carbondale.

McGregor, J. C.
    1965   *Southwestern Archaeology.* University of Illinois Press, Urbana.

McGuire, R. H.
    1982   Problems in Culture History. In *Hohokam and Patayan: Prehistory of Southwestern Arizona,* edited by R. H. McGuire and M. B. Schiffer, pp. 153–222. Academic Press, New York.

McKenna, J. A., and J. K. Swarthout
    1984   *An Archaeological Reconstruction of Piman Households in the Gila Butte-Santan Area.* OCRM Report No. 62. Office of Cultural Resource Management, Arizona State University, Tempe.

Milich, A. R. (translator)
    1966   *Relaciones by Zárate Salmerón.* Horn & Wallace Publishers, Albuquerque, New Mexico.

Mitchell, D. R.
    1989   *Archaeological Investigations at the Grand Canal Ruins: A Classic Period Site in Phoenix, Arizona.* Publications in Archaeology No. 12. Soil Systems, Phoenix, Arizona.

    1994   Reconstruction of the Pueblo Grande Occupation History. In *The Pueblo Grande Project: Feature Descriptions, Chronology, and Site Structure,* edited by D. R. Mitchell, pp. 255–286. Publications in Archaeology No. 20. Soil Systems, Phoenix, Arizona.

Murphy, B. A., R. C. Lange, and W. L. Deaver
1984   Archaeomagnetic Dating of Three Samples from El Polvorón. In *Hohokam Archaeology along the Salt-Gila Aqueduct, Central Arizona Project, Volume IV: Prehistoric Occupation of the Queen Creek Delta,* edited by L. S. Teague and P. L. Crown, pp. 351–354. Archaeological Series No. 150. Arizona State Museum, University of Arizona, Tucson.

Nelson, M. C.
1999   *Mimbres during the Twelfth Century: Abandonment, Continuity, and Reorganization.* University of Arizona Press, Tucson.

Newman, L., and M. K. Woodson
2002   Ceramics. In *Archaeological Investigations at the Sweetwater Site Along State Route 587 on the Gila River Indian Community,* edited by M. K. Woodson, pp. 137–174. P-MIP Technical Report No. 2002-14. Cultural Resources Management Program, Gila River Indian Community, Sacaton, Arizona.

Nials, F. L., D. A. Gregory, and D. A. Graybill
1989   Salt River Streamflow and Hohokam Irrigation Systems. In *The 1982–1984 Excavations at Las Colinas: Environment and Subsistence,* edited by C. A. Heathington and D. A. Gregory, pp. 59–78. Archaeological Series No. 162. Arizona State Museum, University of Arizona, Tucson.

O'Brien, M. J., and D. E. Lewarch
1982   *Plowzone Archaeology: Contributions to Theory and Technique.* Publications in Anthropology No. 27. Vanderbilt University Press, Nashville, Tennessee.

Orton, C.
2000   *Sampling in Archaeology.* Cambridge University Press, Cambridge.

Pailes, R. A.
1972   *An Archaeological Reconnaissance of Southern Sonora and a Reconsideration of the Rio Sonora Culture.* Unpublished Ph.D. dissertation, Department of Anthropology, Southern Illinois University, Carbondale.

1978   The Rio Sonora Culture in Prehistoric Trade Systems. In *Across the Chichimec Sea: Papers in Honor of J. Charles Kelley,* edited by C. L. Riley and B. C. Hedrick, pp. 134–143. Southern Illinois University Press, Carbondale.

Pfefferkorn, I.
1989   *Sonora: A Description of the Province,* translated and annotated by T. E. Treitlein. University of Arizona Press, Tucson.

Randolph, B., J. A. Darling, C. Loendorf, and B. Rockette
2002   Historic Pima Site Structure and the Evolution of the Sacate Site (GR-909), Gila River Indian Community. In *Visible Archaeology on the Gila River Indian Reservation,* P-MIP Report No. 21. Cultural Resource Program, Gila River Indian Community, Sacaton, Arizona.

Ravesloot, J. C. (editor)
1987   *The Archaeology of the San Xavier Bridge Site (AZ BB:13:14), Tucson Basin, Southern Arizona.* Archaeological Series No. 171. Arizona State Museum, University of Arizona, Tucson.

Ravesloot, J. C., A. Lascaux, and J. H. Thiel (editors)
1992   *Archaeological Studies of an Early Twentieth Century Pima Site: AZ U:9:44 (ASM), Maricopa County, Arizona.* Anthropological Field Studies No. 27. Department of Anthropology, Arizona State University, Tempe.

Ravesloot, J. C., and M. R. Waters
2004   Geoarchaeology and Archaeological Site Patterning on the Middle Gila River, Arizona. *Journal of Field Archaeology* 29(1, 2):203–214.

Ravesloot, J. C., and S. M. Whittlesey
1987   Inferring the Protohistoric Period in Southern Arizona. In *The Archaeology of the San Xavier Bridge Site (AZ BB:13:14), Tucson Basin, Southern Arizona, Parts 1 and 2,* edited by J. C. Ravesloot, pp. 81–98. Archaeological Series No. 171. Arizona State Museum, University of Arizona, Tucson.

Redman, C. L.
1987   Surface Collection, Sampling, Research Design. *American Antiquity* 52(3):249–265.

Redman, C. L., and P. J. Watson
1970   Systematic, Intensive Surface Collection. *American Antiquity* 52(2):249–265.

Reff, D. T.
1990   Contact Shock and the Protohistoric Period in the Greater Southwest. In *Perspectives on Southwestern Prehistory*, edited by P. E. Minnis and C. L. Redman, pp. 276–288. Westview Press, Boulder, Colorado.

1991   Anthropological Analysis of Exploration Texts: Cultural Discourse and the Ethnological Import of Fray Marcos de Niza's Journey Cibola. *American Anthropologist* 93(4):636–654.

1992   Contact Shock in Northwestern New Spain, 1518–1764. In *Disease and Demography in the Americas*, edited by J. Verano and D. Ubelaker, pp. 265–276. Smithsonian Institution Press, Washington, D.C.

Rhode, D.
1988   Measurement of Archaeological Diversity and the Sample-Size Effect. *American Antiquity* 53:708–716.

Rice, G. E.
1998a War and Water: An Ecological Perspective on Hohokam Irrigation. *Kiva* 63(3):263–301.

1998b Structuring the Temporal Dimension for Tonto Basin Prehistory. In *A Synthesis of Tonto Basin Prehistory: The Roosevelt Archaeological Studies, 1989 to 1998,* edited by Glen E. Rice, pp. 11–32. Anthropological Field Studies No. 41. Office of Cultural Resource Management, Arizona State University, Tempe.

2001 Warfare and Massing in the Salt and Gila Basins of Central Arizona. In *Deadly Landscapes: Case Studies in Prehistoric Southwestern Warfare*, edited by G. Rice and S. A. LeBlanc. University of Utah Press, Salt Lake City.

Rice, G. E., S. Upham, and L. Nicholas (editors)
1983 *Alicia, The History of a Piman Homestead.* Anthropological Field Studies Report No. 4. Office of Cultural Resource Management, Arizona State University, Tempe.

Riley, C. L.
1976 *Sixteenth Century Trade in the Greater Southwest.* Research Records of the University Museum, Mesoamerican Studies No. 10. Southern Illinois University, Carbondale.

1980 Mesoamerica and the Hohokam: A View from the 16th Century. In *Current Issues in Hohokam Prehistory: A Symposium*, edited by D. E. Doyel and F. Plog, pp. 41–48. Anthropological Research Papers No. 23. Department of Anthropology, Arizona State University, Tempe.

1987 *The Frontier People: The Greater Southwest in the Protohistoric Period.* University of New Mexico Press, Albuquerque.

Roberts, F. H. H.
1935 A Survey of Southwestern Archaeology. *American Anthropologist* 37(1):1–35.

Roberts, H., and R. V. N. Ahlstrom
1997 Malaria, Microbes, and Mechanisms of Change. *Kiva* 63(1):117–135.

Robinson, W. S.
1951 A Method for Chronologically Ordering Archaeological Deposits. *American Antiquity* 16(3):293–301.

Rogers, M. J.
1936 *Yuman Pottery Making.* San Diego Museum Papers No. 2. San Diego Museum, San Diego, California.

Roper, D. C.
1976 Lateral Displacement of Artifacts Due to Plowing. *American Antiquity* 41:372–375.

Rosenthal, J. E., D. Brown, M. Severson, and J. B. Clouts
1978 *The Quijotoa Valley Project.* National Park Service, United States Department of the Interior, Tucson, Arizona.

Russell, F.
1908 *The Pima Indians.* Twenty-sixth Annual Report of the Bureau of American Ethnology, 1904–1905. Report to the Secretary of the Smithsonian Institution, Washington, D.C.

Sauer, C. O.
1932 *The Road to Cibola.* Ibero-Americana III. University of California Press, Berkeley.

Scantling, F. H.
1940 *Excavations at the Jackrabbit Ruin, Papago Indian Reservation, Arizona.* Unpublished M.A. thesis, Department of Anthropology, University of Arizona, Tucson.

Schaafsma, P., and C. L. Riley (editors)
1999 *The Casas Grandes World.* University of Utah Press, Salt Lake City.

Schiffer, M. B.
1972 Archaeological Context and Systematic Context. *American Antiquity* 37:156–165.

1987 *Formation Processes of the Archaeological Record.* University of New Mexico Press, Albuquerque.

Seymour, D.
1989 The Dynamics of Sobaipuri Settlement in the Eastern Pimería Alta. *Journal of the Southwest* 31(2):205–222.

1993 In Search of the Sobaipuri Pima: Archaeology of the Plain and Subtle. *Archaeology in Tucson* 7(1):1–4.

1997 Finding History in the Archaeological Record: The Upper Piman Settlement of Guevavi. *Kiva* 62(3):245–260.

Shenk, L. O., and G. A. Teague
1975 *Excavations at the Tubac Presidio.* Archaeological Series No. 85. Arizona State Museum, University of Arizona, Tucson.

Simon, A. W., J. H. Burton, and D. R. Abbott
1998 Intraregional Connections in the Development and Distribution of Salado Polychromes in Central Arizona. *Journal of Anthropological Research* 54:519–547.

Simpson, K., and S. J. Wells
1983 *Archaeological Survey in the Eastern Tucson Basin, Saguaro National Monument, Rincon Mountain Unit, Cactus Forest Area.* Publications in Anthropology No. 22. Western Archaeological and Conservation Center, Tucson, Arizona.

Sires, E. W.
1984 Excavations at El Polvorón. In *Hohokam Archaeology along the Salt-Gila Aqueduct, Central Arizona Project, Vol. IV, Part II: Prehistoric Occupation of the Queen*

Creek Delta, edited by L. S. Teague and P. L. Crown, pp. 219–354. Archaeological Series No. 150. Arizona State Museum, University of Arizona, Tucson.

Smith, F. J.
1966   The Relación Diaria of Father Kino. In *Father Kino in Arizona*, edited by F. J. Smith, J. L. Kessell, and F. J. Fox, pp. 1–52. Arizona Historical Foundation, Phoenix.

Southworth, C. H.
1914   *Gila River Survey, Pinal County, Arizona.* United States Department of the Interior, United States Indian Service Irrigation, Washington, D.C.

1919   The History of Irrigation along the Gila River. In *Hearings before the Committee on Indian Affairs, House of Representatives, Sixty-Sixth Congress, First Session, on the Condition of the Various Tribes of Indians,* vol. 2, appendix A, pp. 105–225. Government Printing Office, Washington, D.C.

Teague, G. A.
1980   *Reward Mine and Associated Sites, Historical Archaeology on the Papago Reservation.* Publications in Anthropology No. 11. Western Archaeological Center, Tucson, Arizona.

Teague, L. S.
1988   The History of Occupation at Las Colinas. In *The 1982–1984 Excavations at Las Colinas: The Site and Its Features,* edited by D. A. Gregory, W. L. Deaver, S. K. Fish, R. Gardiner, R. W. Layhe, F. L. Nials, and L. S. Teague, pp. 121–152. Archaeological Series No. 162. Arizona State Museum, University of Arizona, Tucson.

1989   The Postclassic and the Fate of the Hohokam. In *The 1982–1984 Excavations at Las Colinas: Syntheses and Conclusions,* edited by L. S. Teague and W. L. Deaver, pp. 145–167. Archaeological Series No. 162. Arizona State Museum, University of Arizona, Tucson.

Trubowitz, N. L.
1978   The Persistence of Settlement Pattern in a Cultivated Field. In *Essays in Northeastern Anthropology in Memory of Marian W. White,* edited by W. Englebrecht and D. Grayson, pp. 41–66. Occasional Publications in Northeastern Anthropology No. 5. Franklin Pierce College, Rindge, New Hampshire.

Upham, S.
1983   Excavation of Alicia. In *Alicia, The History of a Piman Homestead,* edited by G. E. Rice, S. Upham, and L. Nicholas, pp. 85–102. Anthropological Field Studies No. 4. Office of Cultural Resource Management, Arizona State University, Tempe.

Vokes, A.
1984   The Shell Assemblage of the Salt-Gila Aqueduct Project Sites. In *Hohokam Archaeology along the Salt Gila Aqueduct, Central Arizona Project* Archaeological Series No. 150, pp. 465–550. Arizona State Museum, University of Arizona, Tucson.

Wallace, H. D., and W. H. Doelle
  2001   Classic Period Warfare in Southern Arizona. In *Deadly Landscapes: Case Studies in Prehistoric Southwestern Warfare*, edited by G. Rice and S. A. LeBlanc, pp. 239288. University of Utah Press, Salt Lake City.

Wallace, H. D., and J. P. Holmlund
  1986 *Petroglyphs of the Picacho Mountains South Central, Arizona.* Institute for American Research. Anthropological Papers No. 6. Bureau of Reclamation, Phoenix, Arizona.

Walsh-Anduze, M.-E.
  1993 *The Sourcing of Hohokam Red-on-buff Ceramics Using Inductively Coupled Plasma Spectroscopy: "Schist Happens."* Unpublished M.A. thesis, Northern Arizona University, Flagstaff.

  1996a Ceramic Analysis, Areas 15 and 16: Functional, Spatial, and Temporal Associations. In *Life on the Floodplain: Further Investigations at Pueblo Salado for Phoenix Sky Harbor International Airport,* edited by D. H. Greenwald, J. H. Ballagh, D. R. Mitchell, and R. A. Anduze, pp. 85–95. Anthropological Papers No. 4. Pueblo Grande Museum, Phoenix, Arizona.

  1996b Changes in the Structure of Hohokam Ceramic Production: The Results of the Pueblo Salado Area 6 Ceramic Study. In *Life on the Floodplain: Further Investigations at Pueblo Salado for Phoenix Sky Harbor International Airport,* edited by D. H. Greenwald, J. H. Ballagh, D. R. Mitchell, and R. A. Anduze, pp. 97–140. Anthropological Papers No. 4. Pueblo Grande Museum, Phoenix, Arizona.

Waters, M. R.
  1982   The Lowland Patayan Ceramic Tradition. In *Hohokam and Patayan: Prehistory of Southwestern Arizona,* edited by R. H. McGuire and M. B. Schiffer, pp. 275–297. Academic Press, New York.

Waters, M. R., and J. C. Ravesloot
  2001   Landscape Change and the Cultural Evolution of the Hohokam along the Middle Gila River and Other River Valleys in Southern Arizona. *American Antiquity* 66(2):285–299.

Waugh, R. J.
  1995 *Plainware Ceramics from the Midden at Presidio Santa Cruz de Terrenate, Arizona.* Unpublished M.A. thesis, Department of Anthropology, University of Arizona, Tucson.

  2002 Protohistoric and Early Historical-period Plainwares on the Pimería Alta. Unpublished paper presented at the annual meeting of the Society for Historical Archaeology, Providence, Rhode Island.

Wenker, C. T., D. H. Greenwald, and R. A. Anduze
1996   Excavation Results, Area 6. In *Life on the Floodplain: Further Investigations at Pueblo Salado for Phoenix Sky Harbor International Airport: Data Recovery and Re-evaluation, Volume 2, Part 1, The Report,* edited by D. H. Greenwald, J. H. Ballagh, D. R. Mitchell, and R. A. Anduze, pp. 33–83. Anthropological Papers No. 4. Pueblo Grande Museum, Phoenix, Arizona.

Wheat, J. B.
1956   A Review of "The Sobaípuri Indians of the Upper San Pedro Valley, Southeastern Arizona," by Charles C. Di Peso. *American Antiquity* 21:430–431.

Whittaker, J. C.
1984   *Arrowheads and Artisans: Stone Tool Manufacture and Individual Variation at Grasshopper Pueblo.* Unpublished Ph.D. dissertation, Department of Anthropology, University of Arizona, Tucson.

Whittlesey, S. M.
1982   Vessel Thinning Techniques and Ethnic Identification. In *Cholla Project Archaeology,* edited by J. J. Reid, pp. 18–21. Archaeological Series No. 161. Arizona State Museum, University of Arizona, Tucson.

1986   Restorable and Partial Vessels. In *Archaeological Investigations at AZ U:14:75 (ASM), A Turn of the Century Pima Homestead,* edited by R. W. Layhe, pp. 74–101. Archaeological Series No. 172. Arizona State Museum, University of Arizona, Tucson.

1996   Culture History: Prehispanic Narratives for Southern Arizona. In *Background and Research Design for Prehistoric Archaeological Resources,* by C. Van West and S. Whittlesey, pp. 45–80. Statistical Research, Tucson, Arizona.

1997a Native American Ceramics. In *Pithouse, Presidio, and Privy: 1,400 Years of Archaeology and History on Block 180, Tucson, AZ,* edited by R. Ciolek-Torrello and M. T. Swanson, pp. 421–468. Technical Series No. 63. Statistical Research, Tucson, Arizona.

1997b Cultural Affiliation, Population Movement, and Migration. In *Vanishing River: Landscapes and Lives of the Lower Verde Valley: The Lower Verde Archaeological Project,* edited by S. M. Whittlesey, R. Ciolek-Torrello, and J. H. Altschul, pp. 672–689. Statistical Research, Tucson, Arizona.

Wilcox, D. R.
1987   New Models of Social Structure at the Palo Parado Site. In *The Hohokam Village: Site Structure and Organization,* edited by D. E. Doyel, pp. 223–248. American Association for the Advancement of Science, Glenwood Springs, Colorado.

1991   The Mesoamerican Ballgame in the American Southwest. In *The Mesoamerican Ballgame,* edited by V. L. Scarborough and D. R. Wilcox, pp. 101–125. University of Arizona Press, Tucson.

Wilcox, D. R., T. R. McGuire, and C. Sternberg
   1981   *Snaketown Revisited: A Partial Cultural Resource Survey, Analysis of Site Structure, and an Ethnohistoric Study of the Proposed Hohokam-Pima National Monument.* Archaeological Series No. 155. Arizona State Museum, University of Arizona, Tucson.

Wilcox, D. R., and W. B. Masse (editors)
   1981   *The Protohistoric Period in the North American Southwest, AD 1450–1700.* Anthropological Research Papers No. 24. Department of Anthropology, Arizona State University, Tempe.

Wilcox, D. R., and L. O. Shenk
   1977   *The Architecture of Casa Grande and Its Interpretation.* Archaeological Series No. 115. Arizona State Museum, University of Arizona, Tucson.

Williams, J.
   1986   The Presidio of Santa Cruz de Terrenate: A Forgotten Fortress of Southern Arizona. *The Smoke Signal* 47–48:129–146.

Wilson, J. P.
   1999   *Peoples of the Middle Gila: A Documentary History of the Pimas and Maricopas, 1500s–1945.* Unpublished manuscript on file, Cultural Resource Management Program, Gila River Indian Community, Sacaton, Arizona.

Windes, T.
   1977   Typology and Technology of Anasazi Ceramics. In *Settlement and Subsistence along the Lower Chaco River: The CGP Survey,* edited by C. A. Reher, pp. 279–370. University of New Mexico Press, Albuquerque.

Winter, J. C.
   1973   Cultural Modifications of the Gila Pima: A.D. 1697– A.D. 1846. *Ethnohistory* 20(1):67–77.

Withers, A. M.
   1941   Excavations at Valshni Village, Papago Indian Reservation, Arizona. Unpublished M.A. thesis, Department of Anthropology, University of Arizona, Tucson.

Wolfman, D.
   1984   Geomagnetic Dating Methods in Archaeology. *Advances in Archaeological Method and Theory* 7:363–458.

Wood, J. S.
   1987   Checklist of Pottery Types for the Tonto National Forest: An Introduction to the Archaeological Ceramics of Central Arizona. *The Arizona Archaeologist* 21. The Arizona Archaeological Society, Phoenix.

Wood, W. R., and D. L. Johnson
 1978   A Survey of Disturbance Processes in Archaeological Site Formation. In *Advances in Archaeological Method and Theory*, vol. 1, edited by M. Schiffer, pp. 315–381. Academic Press, New York.

Woodson, M. K.
 2002   Synthesis. In *Archaeological Investigations at the Sweetwater Site along State Route 587 on the Gila River Indian Community*, edited by M. K. Woodson, pp. 212–234. CRMP Technical Report No. 2002-14. Cultural Resources Management Program, Gila River Indian Community, Sacaton, Arizona.

Woodson, M. K. (editor)
 2002   *Archaeological Investigations at the Sweetwater Site along State Route 587 on the Gila River Indian Community*. CRMP Technical Report No. 2002-14. Cultural Resources Management Program, Gila River Indian Community, Sacaton, Arizona.

Woodson, M. K, and D. Morgan
 2002   Data Recovery Results. In *Archaeological Investigations at the Sweetwater Site along State Route 587 on the Gila River Indian Community*, edited by M. K. Woodson, pp. 58–120. CRMP Technical Report No. 2002-14. Cultural Resources Management Program, Gila River Indian Community, Sacaton, Arizona.

Zyniecki, M.
 1993   The Chronology of the Polvorón Phase. In *Early Desert Farming: Archaeological Investigations in the Phoenix Sky Harbor Center: Special Studies, Synthesis, and Conclusions*, edited by D. H. Greenwald and J. H. Ballagh, pp. 141–150. Anthropological Research Paper No. 17. SWCA, Flagstaff, Arizona.